TWAYNE'S WORLD AUTHORS SERIES

A Survey of the World's Literature

Sylvia E. Bowman, Indiana University

GENERAL EDITOR

FRANCE

Maxwell A. Smith, Guerry Professor of French, Emeritus
The University of Chattanooga
Former Visiting Professor in Modern Languages
The Florida State University

EDITOR

Paul Scarron

(TWAS 194)

TWAYNE'S WORLD AUTHORS SERIES (TWAS)

The purpose of TWAS is to survey the major writers—novelists, dramatists, historians, poets, philosophers, and critics—of the nations of the world. Among the national literatures covered are those of Australia, Canada, China, Eastern Europe, France, Germany, Greece, India, Italy, Japan, Latin America, the Netherlands, New Zealand, Poland, Russia, Scandinavia, Spain, and the African nations, as well as Hebrew, Yiddish, and Latin Classical literatures. This survey is complemented by Twayne's United States Authors Series and English Authors Series.

The intent of each volume in these series is to present a critical-analytical study of the works of the writer; to include biographical and historical material that may be necessary for understanding, appreciation, and critical appraisal of the writer; and to present all material in clear, concise English—but not to vitiate the scholarly content of the work by doing so.

Paul Scarron

By FREDERICK A. de ARMAS
Louisiana State University

Twayne Publishers, Inc.   : :   New York

MANUFACTURED IN THE UNITED STATES OF AMERICA

Twayne 11/77 2360

Preface

One of the most conspicuous literary figures of the seventeenth century was Paul Scarron. French students are apt to remember him as a man who did not follow the trends of Classicism prevalent in that country at the time; as a "grotesque" figure, literally and as defined by the Romantic school. Paul Scarron, a handsome and lively youth, was stricken at an early age by a paralyzing and deforming illness. Just as he found himself free from the domineering environment of his home the unforeseen illness which lasted all his life became as great a tyrant as his stepmother.

The French poet once described the effects of his illness: "My legs and my thighs made at first an obtuse angle, then a right angle and now an acute one. My thighs and my body make another, and my head leans over my stomach. I am not unlike the letter Z. I have shortened arms as well as legs, and fingers as well as arms. Indeed I am an abstract of all human misery." Yet, such great sufferings did not seem to affect his character. Indeed, prominent Parisians flocked to his home to see a man in such a miserable condition be able to converse as wittily as anyone in the kingdom. Literary figures admired his talent, while courtiers praised his wit. Scarron, then, is remembered as a human being persecuted by fortune, who lashed out against it with satire and invective. The name Scarron is synonymous with the burlesque. Scarron deserved the title of leader of the burlesque movement mainly for his poetry and conversation. His contemporaries were diverted by Scarron's travesty of Virgil's *Aeneid,* and for his satire against mythology in *Typhon.* Yet, these works are not read today. What we remember Scarron for, is his one novel, the *Roman comique* which ranks second only to *La Princesse de Clèves* in the novelistic production of the seventeenth century. Some of his plays like *Dom Japhet d'Arménie* are also enjoyed today. Yet, despite the fact that his burlesque works have fallen into oblivion, critics insist on discussing only the burlesque elements present in the French poet's works. The *Roman comique* and the plays are subjected to one-sided criticism, while all other elements are disregarded. Emile Magne, Scarron's most prominent biographer, discussing the interpolated stories in the *Roman comique,* considers them deplorable. The lack of unity of the novel, its picaresque and burlesque tendencies, are aired, while all other elements are discarded. The same critical technique has been applied to his theater. Most of Scarron's plays are based on Spanish *comedias* which contain many romanesque elements: disguises, chance encounters in the night, unknown ladies, duels, recognitions, and so on. Yet, his plays are often classified as burlesque. Robert Berens, for example, in his study on satire, discards the romanesque elements: "Scarron wanted to give the public what it liked." He, like critics of the *Roman comique,* sees all such tendencies as "concessions" to the tastes of the time, without considering the possibility that it was the public that demanded the burlesque and that Scarron's "concessions" may have been to this tendency.

One of the purposes of this work is then to re-evaluate the writings of Scarron. The often praised poet of the burlesque had a bent for the romanesque. As his life progressed, and his interest in literature became something other than just the possibility of earning a livelihood through it, the romanesque tastes of the French poet began to develop. In his works we can trace such an evolution from the burlesque to the romanesque. A combination of the comical and the ideal is what attracts the reader to the works of this author. Scarron knows how to laugh at life's contingencies; but he can also pursue the truly ideal, devoid of the affectations of the *précieuses* exemplified in novels such as *La Clélie.*

In addition to re-evaluating the works of Scarron, this book will attempt to present to the American reader a picture as complete as possible of the life and writings of this French author. Although there is one biography available in English to the public, there is no general study of Paul Scarron available in this language; in fact, such a survey has not been attempted even in French.

The prose quotations are given in English in my own translation, except those of the *Roman comique.* For the novel, the seventeenth-century translation of Tom Brown has been used. The poetry is given in the original, but is followed by an English translation. Portions of the third chapter are based on the author's *The Four Interpolated Stories in the Roman Comique: Their Sources and Unifying Function.*

I would like to take this opportunity to thank Professor George B. Daniel for his encouragement and suggestions. He first introduced me to Paul Scarron. I would also like to thank Professor Robert Chumbley for his help in translation: much of the quoted poetry was translated by him. I would also like to thank Mrs. Jane Kleiner, interlibrary loan librarian at Louisiana State University, Professor Gary Rodgers, and Mr. Carl Wilkins, for their help.

.

Contents

Chronology

1610   Birth of Paul Scarron. Baptized at the church of Saint-Sulpice.

1613   Gabrielle Goguet, Paul's mother, dies.

1617   Françoise de Plaix becomes Paul Scarron's stepmother.

1623   Spent with a relative at Charleville.

1624   Enters an academy in Paris.

1629   Assumes the *petit collet*.

1631   Publishes his first poem as a *pièce liminaire* in Scudéry's tragicomedy, *Lygdamon et Lydias*.

1633   Secretary to Charles de Beaumanoir, bishop of Le Mans.

1635   Trip to Rome where Paul Scarron meets the painter Nicolas Poussin. Returns the same year.

1636   Given a prebend in the Chapter of Saint-Julien in Le Mans but must fight for it.

1637   Induced by the count of Belin, Scarron writes pamphlets against Pierre Corneille. The count dies as well as his other protector, the bishop of Le Mans.

1638   Beginnings of the crippling disease which will remain with him throughout his life.

1640   The *procès* over the prebend ends in Scarron's favor. Meets Marie de Hautefort who has been exiled to Le Mans by Richelieu. Scarron's father has also been exiled from Paris by the cardinal, and the poet journeys to the capital to intercede in his favor. He then decides to settle in Paris.

1642   Journeys to the baths at Bourbon-l'Archambault to seek relief from his illness. Writes the first *Légende de Bourbon* in memory of the baths. He also writes the *Requeste du petit Scarron au Grand Cardinal* and a second *Légende de Bourbon*, dealing with his second trip to the baths.

1643   *Recueils des quelques vers burlesques* published by Toussainct Quinet. This begins the "Marquisat de Quinet." His first play, *Jodelet ou le maître valet* is a tremendous success.

1644   Publishes the *Suite des oeuvres burlesques* and the *Typhon*, dedicated to Mazarin.

1645   *Jodelet ou le maître valet* published. Presents *Les trois Dorotées*.

1646   Six-week trip to Le Mans.

1647   Publishes *Les trois Dorotées ou le Jodelet souffleté; La suite des oeuvres burlesques, seconde partie; La relation véritable* where he mentions for the first time his intention to write a novel about Le Mans; and *Les Boutades du Capitaine Matamore*.

1648 The Fronde erupts. Begins publication of *Le Virgile Travesti.*
1649 Publishes Book V of the *Virgile Travesti* where he condemns the burlesque.
1650 Meets Françoise d'Aubigné. Led by Cabart de Villermont, Scarron becomes involved in the Société des Indes Equinoxiales and plans to migrate to America. Publishes *L'Héritier ridicule.*
1651 Publishes the *Mazarinade,* the first part of the *Roman comique,* and *Les Oeuvres burlesques, troisième partie.*
1652 Marries Françoise d'Aubigné and leaves for Touraine, fearing reprisals from Mazarin.
1653 Returns to Paris and publishes *Dom Japhet d'Arménie.*
1654 Quarrels with Boisrobert over *L'Ecolier de Salamanque.* Scarron's play is presented at the Marais while Boisrobert's appears at the Hôtel de Bourgogne. Finishes the second part of the *Roman comique.*
1655 The quarrel extends to Boisrobert's brother, d'Ouville. Scarron begins the publication of the *Nouvelles tragi-comiques.* Receives a pension from Nicolas Foucquet to whom he dedicates *Le guardien de soy-même.* Creates a *Gazette burlesque* which is interrupted at the end of the year.
1656 Completes a tragicomedy of Tristan l'Hermite, *Les Coups de l'amour et de la fortune.* Publishes the ode, *Léandre et Héro,* and the play *Le Marquis ridicule.*
1657 Publishes the second part of the *Roman comique.* Meets Christina of Sweden.
1658 Experiments with alchemy.
1659 Retires to the country where he completes *La Fausse apparence* and *Le Prince corsaire.*
1660 Returns to Paris. Dies on 5 or 6 October.
1663 Guillaume de Luyne publishes *La Fausse apparence, Le Prince corsaire,* and three unfinished plays by Scarron.

CHAPTER 1

Scarron's Life

I Scarron's youth (1610–1629)

HENRY IV was dead. Like his immediate predecessor, he had been assassinated. Riding in a carriage through Paris, the Warrior King was stabbed to death by a fanatic called Ravaillac. With his death ends a bloody and chaotic period in French history that witnessed the constant wars between Catholic and Protestant factions which culminated in the celebrated Saint Bartholomew's Day massacre. With Louis XIII and his successor Louis XIV, France would enter a new period that has been designated as "an epoch of order, of discipline."[1] This new era would be mirrored in its literature through the Neoclassic movement; and France would become the cultural center of Europe.

The people, tired of the rigors and uncertainties of war, attempted to purify their spirits and their language. Reacting against the passions elicited throughout the bellicose sixteenth century, the men of the seventeenth became introspective, impassive, and rational, establishing a formalized political structure that would prevent further internal conflicts. These structures are also found in the literature, where the newly created French Academy imposed rules on the writers of the time; best known are the unities in Neoclassical tragedy.

Only four days after the funeral procession marched through Paris mourning the death of Henry IV, on July 4, 1610, Paul Scarron was baptized with his father's name at the church of Saint-Sulpice.[2] Paul would grow up in this new epoch, and yet he would never be fully a part of it. This does not mean that he looked backward to the preceding period; he was a fervent admirer of the new formalism, and would defend the poet Malherbe, who in Boileau's famous couplet brought to the French language for the first time a sense of proper cadence, against his father's arguments. His father preferred the poetry of Ronsard, the great sixteenth-century poet and leader of the Pléiade whose flamboyance and flowery style were typical of the previous age.

Paul Scarron, father, was a counselor in the Parlement of Paris and thus belonged to the nobility of the robe. The mother, Gabrielle Goguet, a tender woman, died three years after the birth of her son Paul, so that the poet remembered very little of her. Paul was the seventh of eight children. However, only two in addition to him survived their childhood: Anne and Françoise.

The harmony of childhood was further disturbed when the father presented them with a stepmother: Françoise de Plaix. This woman loved domination of other people, delighted in dispute, and could not tolerate the children. This situation became intolerable when the new Mme Scarron gave birth to her own children, three of whom survived.

Anne, Françoise, and Paul could not turn to their father. The arrogant and boisterous counselor gave in to his new wife and became resigned and quiet at home, allowing Mme Scarron to run the household. She gambled, and usually she lost; but her extravagance outside the home was only translated into avarice, for which the whole family suffered. Naomi F. Phelps, in her biography of Paul Scarron, includes the following anecdote: "In fact, his wife dominated him so completely that once when she was very ill, her husband, who had been convinced by her that he was poverty-stricken, was so terrified at the thought that he would be a penniless widower that he begged her to leave him a pension of six hundred livres after her death—this in spite of the fact that his annual income represented a considerable fortune at that time."[3]

Mrs. Phelps also attributes to his domineering wife the counselor's mania about Saint Paul which earned him the title of "the Apostle." He would recite the Epistles everywhere he went and to anyone that might listen. Other biographers, however, contend that his interest in Saint Paul was present before their marriage.[4] Anyway, this was not the only eccentricity of the counselor: he would also dress in the fashion of the court of Henry II. It may be that these practices were a reaction to his new wife: he exhibited the patience of a Saint Paul, while looking longingly at the happy days that were past.

The Scarron household was then run by the domineering second wife of the counselor to the detriment of all. No one attempted to do anything about it except the young poet. It was at this early age that Paul Scarron had his first lesson on the burlesque.[5]

There is little a young boy may do to counter an adverse home environment, but the poet discovered that laughter and satire were effective weapons, first to keep from suffering, and second to inflict the only punishment he was able on those that deserved it: and what more effective target for satire than a woman whose avarice at home only served to provide her with means to gamble, while her children lacked many necessities?

Thus, some traits of his writings are already evident: he believes in the clarity, preciseness, and formality of the French language, opposing the views of the counselor. In this sense, he is a Classical author. However, he sees the realities of life, and laughter as a method of combat. Although he will admire the lofty ideals of many Neoclassic authors and abide by their formalism, he will never forget the realities, and he will juxtapose laughter to the impossible dream.

To preserve peace in the household, the Apostle exiled his own son. He sent him to live with some relatives in Charleville, where Paul spent his thirteenth and fourteenth years. Upon his return home he was not cured from that malady of the burlesque. In fact, if anything, he was more adept in its use. His parents then sent him to an Academy in Paris; there, Paul Scarron acquired a hatred toward pedantry and a basic knowledge of Latin.[6]

To escape the bleakness and boredom of the Academy the young poet began to read fiction from Spain. This action was to have a definite influence in his life and writings, since he would use many Spanish sources in composing his mature works. This influence would be felt not only in the composition of his theatrical pieces but also in prose fiction and poetry. He probably read *comedias* from the chief Spanish playwrights of the time: Lope de Vega, Tirso de Molina, and others. Undoubtedly, he read Cervantes' *Don Quijote* which had been recently translated into the French by César Oudin and François de Rosset, as well as his *Novelas ejemplares,* which had also been translated by Rosset and Vital d'Audigier. If he read any picaresque novels at this time, they might have reminded him of his plight. In sum, Paul Scarron became acquainted at this time with the diverse literary forms prevalent in Spain during its period of greatest literary glory: the Golden Age.

At the age of nineteen, Paul Scarron escaped the Academy and began to versify, since he found himself free to do as he chose in the glittering Paris of Louis XIII. Meanwhile, his father had been deliberating as to what road his son should take. He realized that the temperament of the young Scarron was not fit for Parlement. Anyway, the avaricious stepmother would not have allowed her husband to spend as much money as was required to obtain such an office. Counselor Scarron acted in a very wise manner when he chose the church for his son. In 1629 Paul assumed the *petit collet* and became an *abbé*. According to Cosnac, the *petit collet* is the necessary passport of men of letters in the *grand monde,* since it allows poets to enter the salons and *ruelles,* while imposing on them no duties or restrictions.[7]

II *From Paris to Le Mans* (1629–1635)

The *petit collet* was only a first step until ecclesiastical employment or benefits could be obtained. In the meantime, Paul Scarron enjoyed an allowance from his father and the freedom to exercise his knack for the burlesque and his desire to be a poet in the city of Paris.

Although he wore the *petit collet,* he did not think of adopting the austere manner of churchmen; in this he followed the example of many of his contemporaries. According to Emile Magne, his unhappy childhood lacking in parental affection drove him to the sensual life. Magne also states that his early verse records the many loves he had. Iris, Philis, Cloris, and Silvie are some of the fictitious names he gave those women for whom he agonized, and even "died" of love, according to the customs of the time.[8]

His love adventures and duels somewhat parallel the Spanish *novelas* he had probably read. As opposed to the French heroic novels, Spanish *novelas* treated romantic incidents that may appear fictional to a modern reader but that seemed very real to the adventuresome gallants of Paris and Madrid in the seventeenth century. One such incident recounted by Magne may remind the reader of an interpolated story in his *Roman comique,* the story of The Invisible Mistress, since it deals with an assignation with an unknown lady.

One day the young poet received a letter from an unknown lady declaring that she was aware of his merit and that she wanted to meet him. She stated that at a certain hour he should wait for her at the faubourg Saint-Germain. He did, and no one came. Three other letters were received, and three times the young poet was deceived. He finally discovered it had all been a joke played on him by his friend Armand de Madaillan. Yet the fact remains that he was ready to partake of any adventure—the more mysterious the better. This taste for the romanesque was as I stated before, very Spanish, and showed in Scarron a trait very different from his usual satire and mordant humor: this must be particularly remembered in any discussion of his *Roman comique* since, as mentioned before, a similar incident occurs in it. Théophile Gautier sums up the character of the poet when he states that his prevalent humors at this time are the sanguine and the bilious.[9] The first accounts for his propensities for the romanesque; the second for his satiric wit and belligerent spirit. This last one brought him very close to Paul de Gondi, later to become the famous Cardinal de Retz.[10] Scarron also counted as friends many of the writers of the time. Voiture, Mairet, Rotrou, and Saint-Amant were among his acquaintances. He also frequented the theaters: the Marais and the Hôtel de Bourgogne, where he met many of the actors and actresses, who in the seventeenth century were not highly regarded. In fact, some had no home and tried to find places to stay when a performance was over. No one believed in the dignity of the theatrical profession, and many thought they were thieves and debauched beings; but Scarron, knowing them intimately, will devote his *Roman comique* to their trials, tribulations, and love affairs.

From the theater, Scarron would go to the salons. He was known to have frequented the salon of Marion de Lorme who had gained fame from her distinguished lovers: Richelieu, Cinq-Mars, Saint-Evremond, and Buckingham, to name a few. Thus, from his nineteenth to his twenty-third year, Paul Scarron roamed through Paris meeting all its people and becoming acquainted with human nature in all its aspects, his bent for the theater and for poetry, slowly growing strong. It was during this epoch that Scarron was introduced to Georges de Scudéry, the famous author of heroic novels and tragicomedies. In 1631 Scudéry had published his first tragicomedy, *Lygdamon et Lydias,* and in it our poet published a *pièce liminaire,* which was his first printed work.

The careless years, however, had to end. Françoise de Plaix, tired of seeing her husband's income go to the "debauched" son from a first marriage, insisted that the father find him a position. The counselor had a cousin, Pierre Scarron, who was bishop of Grenoble. It may have been through him that he gained a position for his son as secretary to the bishop of Maine, Charles

de Beaumanoir. At twenty-three Scarron felt he was too young
to give up the pleasures of the capital. However, he had no choice.
He was soon in the city of Le Mans, where the bishop awaited
him. Parisians regarded the rest of the inhabitants of France as
uncultured provincials who clumsily tried without success to imitate the manners of the great city, and the customs of the people
in the provinces immediately alarmed Scarron: the ladies had
nothing of the coquettes in Paris, and they dressed very inappro-
priately. However, his dealings with the bishop served to attenuate
the shock of his new surroundings, since Charles de Beaumanoir
appreciated the humor and *joie de vivre* of the Parisian poet. Luckily, the poet's stay in Le Mans was interrupted by an agreeable
trip to Rome in 1635.

III *The Italian Sojourn (1635)*

The king was sending to Rome a secret mission headed by the
archbishop of Lyons and brother of the Cardinal Richelieu,
Alphonse de Richelieu. His purpose was to persuade the pope
to dissolve the marriage between Gaston d'Orléans and Marguerite
de Laurraine Vaudement, contracted in secrecy three years previously. This, however, although ostensibly the purpose of the
mission, was really not the only preoccupation of the French prelates that were going to Rome: most were trying to improve their
position, including Charles de Beaumanoir, who dreamed of
becoming archbishop of Lyons, thus replacing Alphonse de
Richelieu. Only Scarron had no other preoccupation than to have
a good time in a city he had heard rivaled even Paris in its luxuries
and gaiety.

Among the people he met in Rome were the physician Bourdelot
and the poet François Maynard.[11] With these friends he under-
took to discover all the "beauties" of Rome. The monuments and
antiquities of the ancient city were almost forgotten at the expense
of brilliant soirees and secret rendezvous.

Only one sonnet, according to Magne, Morillot, Chardon, and
Phelps, gives the reader Scarron's impressions of Rome.[12]

> *Superbes Monuments de l'orgueil des Humains,*
> *Pyramides, Tombeaux, dont la vaine structure*
> *A témoigné que l'Art par l'adresse des mains,*
> *Et l'assidu travail peut vaincre la nature!*

Vieux Palais ruiné, Chef-d'oeuvres des Romains,
Et les derniers efforts de leur Architecture,
Colisée, où souvent ces Peuples inhumains,
De s'entre-assassiner se donnoient tablature.

Par l'injure des ans vous êtes abolis,
Ou du moins la plupart vous êtes démolis!
Il n'est point de ciment que le temps ne dissoude.

Si vos Marbres si durs ont senti son pouvoir,
Dois'je trouver mauvais qu'un méchant Pourpoint noir
Qui m'a duré deux ans, soit percé par le coude?[13]

(Superb monuments of human pride,/pyramids, tombs, whose vain struc-
ture/has shown that Art through manual skills/and assiduous work can
conquer nature!/Old ruined palaces, masterpieces of the Romans,/and
the last efforts of their architecture/the Coliseum, where often these inhuman
people,/abandoned themselves to a merry chase and killed each other./
You have been abolished by the ravages of time,/or at least you have been
mostly demolished!/There is no cement that time won't dissolve./If marble
so solid has felt its power,/should I feel bad when a mischievous black
doublet/which has lasted me two years, tears at the elbow?)

This sonnet, then, represents the only and basic proof for Scarron's
dislike of Rome. It is my belief that such interpretation and particularly the statements by Magne[14] represent a simplistic conception
of Scarron's art and its relation to the burlesque. Such an interpretation is inextricably tied to the poet's character. Thus, I will
try to amend such an interpretation using as a basis both the sonnet
and the poet's character as shown in his actions in Rome.

First, the sonnet does not necessarily represent Scarron's view
of Rome. Magne, Phelps, and Chardon do not realize that this
sonnet is not necessarily derived from his visit to that city;[15] in fact,
it was probably not written at this time since it is an almost exact
translation of a sonnet by the greatest Spanish playwright of the
Golden Age: Lope Félix de Vega Carpio.[16]

At this time, Scarron had not as yet begun to use Spanish literature as the basis for his work. Eight to ten years later this will
happen. It is then probable that this poem was not translated
until much later. It is very unlikely that Scarron would be translating a Spanish poem while visiting Rome, and it is certainly
misleading to judge that a translation necessarily expresses the
thoughts of the translator.[17]

It is also very possible that, for Scarron, Rome was a fascinating city. What could be more romanesque than a rendezvous by some of the ancient ruins? In the *Roman comique,* Rome actually appears as a city filled with mystery and romance. It is in Rome that Destin, the hero of the novel, meets Estoile. In the Platonic tradition it is his destiny to follow his star wheresoever she might lead him. The *Roman comique,* a work saturated with humor, becomes a serious exercise in the romanesque when the setting is Rome.

Finally, a few words about the author should serve to dispel the notion that Scarron had to turn all that is ideal and beautiful into satire. One day, on his voyage of discovery in Rome, accompanied by Bourdelot and Roland Fréart,[18] Scarron happened to meet Nicolas Poussin, the exemplary Classical painter. The intellectuality of his compositions that harmonized a Classical concept of the human form as derived from Raphael with an idealized vision of the grandeurs of the Roman past, struck the imagination of Paul Scarron, who immediately considered him the Malherbe of painting. The artist was at the same time absorbed in the composition of the *Seven Sacraments.* Nevertheless, he received his guests pleasantly. Nicolas Poussin considered Scarron as a typical inhabitant of Le Mans and could not understand his humor. The young poet understood the great genius of Poussin but felt that the Classical artist lacked the dimension of reality and humor which he tried to convey to him. J. J. Jusserand expresses the result of this meeting very clearly: "Scarron thought he would be of service to Poussin in making him laugh, and he never forgot to send him any new book of his which he considered a laughable one. Poussin, in his turn, being asked by Scarron for a picture would paint a bacchanal, but Scarron preferred to obtain from the high-minded artist something in his highest style and he insisted upon Poussin painting for him a *Ravissement de Saint Paul.*[19]

It is sad to read of the boundless admiration that Scarron had for Poussin and of the latter's total distaste for the worldly poet. At a later date Scarron sends Poussin his *Typhon* and threatens him with his *Virgile travesti.* Poussin can only express the "disgust"[20] he has for such works and the hope that Scarron would not send him others like it.

Thus, Poussin took offense when Scarron only wanted him to laugh. The worldly poet wants everyone to share the energy of life in its laughter. Yet, he also understands the great intellectual conceptions and the high ideals of mankind. In fact, he shares them in his admiration for the great Classical artists. Laughter and humor do not mean, in Scarron, a distaste for the ideal. J.J. Jusserand states in this connection: "For all the travesty he put on the shoulders of Virgil, he none the less at bottom adored him, as everybody did in his day. His work was a joke, and he wanted his readers to take it as nothing more than a gaminerie. He knew full well, and was ready to recognize that if it was to be considered in any other light it could not but appear sacrilegious."[21]

In fact, later in life, he would not be angered by Père Vavasseur's statement against the burlesque, and he felt contrite for the "sin" of having originated, or so he thought, a style that would reach epidemic proportions as a reaction against the lofty heights of Classicism.

Thus, Paul Scarron had a fuller vision of life, in a sense, than Poussin and the Classical authors. He saw their vision and admired it. He was a Classicist in his aspirations. Yet early in life he had learned a lesson in survival. Life is not all harmony. The only manner to combat the opposing forces, is to reaffirm what one feels: the great power which is life. Humor then has in him a certain Rabelaisian characteristic since it expresses the will to live fully especially when this is threatened. It is this vigorous strain of vital life which overflows from his clear and concise style that makes him a revolutionary in his epoch. He overturns Classicism by expanding it. His humor, then, is not a negation of the values of his contemporaries, as most of the critics of Scarron affirm. He does not want to ridicule Virgil, and thus he could not understand Poussin's reaction. If at times there is ridicule in the works of Scarron, and bitter ridicule at that, it is not directed at the aspirations of the human race. It is directed against those who do not understand such aspirations: his stepmother, Mme Bouvillon, and certainly Ragotin.

Scarron enjoyed his stay in Rome. In this great monument of human achievement, he walked through its ruins and admired them through the vision of Poussin. He recognized its mystery, and its romanesque possibilities as later expressed in the *Roman comique*. He also enjoyed himself to the fullest in his nightly escapades and bacchic feasts. His humor was such that even the archbishop of Lyons gave him permission to express anything that might enter into his mind since it always amused the churchman. On August 26, he went to his last party in Rome, this one offered by the ambassador de Noailles. Since it was very warm the tables were set in a grotto freshened by twelve fountains, and the wine was chilled by mountain snow.

The *Gazette de France* announced that the travelers left Rome in September. Scarron must again leave the pleasures of the city and return to the provinces.

IV *Le Mans: The Conception of a Novel* (1635–1640)

Having returned to Le Mans, Scarron patiently resumed his routine. He was not a man, however, to let life slip quietly by. Even in a small town of the provinces, there must be places to go where the cosmopolitan atmosphere could be recaptured.

First, the bishop of Le Mans, as stated before, helped to assuage Scarron's nostalgia for the city. Although living in the provinces, the bishop was one of the most notorious gourmets of France. Together with the count d'Olonne, the commandeur de Souvré, and sometimes the marquis de Bois Dauphin, he formed the famous "Ordre des Trois Coteaux," that counted among its members Saint-Evremond who reputedly wrote a one-act play about the society in 1665.[22]

The bishop's family, the Lavardins, also helped Scarron to adjust to this new environment. They appreciated the poet's wit as much as he appreciated the bishop's table. At their *château* of Malicorne and at their *hôtel* in town, Scarron was always welcome. Here he was able to renew his acquaintance with the poet Tristan l'Hermite.

The countess of Soissons, protectress of Rotrou and Louis de Mollier, was also visited by the bishop de Beaumanoir and his young secretary. More important, however, the Bishop also introduced the young poet to François d'Averton, count of Belin, who had in Maine four castles, each designed for different types of pleasures. The friendship that ensued between Scarron and the count, as well as the poet's deep admiration for him, has been immortalized in the *Roman comique* where the count appears as the count d'Orsé.

In addition to these aristocratic pleasures, Paul Scarron also enjoyed, accompanied by Charles Rosteau, a doctor of the Lavardin family, occasional escapades to the inns of Le Mans where they would conduct bacchic feasts and at times create attachments with some of the females present.[23] The young poet was then acquainted with the different facets of life in the province of Maine. And, according to Magne, it is very possible that a troupe of actors stopped at the inn, and that it is this troupe that Scarron used in composing his novel.[24] In any case, the *Roman comique* has been called a novel of manners. If this is true, the milieu of Le Mans is vital to its composition.

In the midst of all these delights of the country, Scarron must have been very worried as to his position. He was dependent on the bishop and had no money of his own. He must have been relieved when a vacancy occurred in the Chapter of Saint-Julien in December, 1636, and the bishop commanded its members to receive Paul Scarron as a canon in possession of a prebend. However, he was suddenly stopped by legal entanglements and was not able to take possession of it until three years later.

The next two years were not very happy ones. In 1637, deprived of his prebend, Scarron sought to gain more influence with his protector, the count of Belin, who was greatly interested in literature: he was the benefactor of Mondory. Although Scarron approved of some of the count's literary ideas such as his dislike for the dramatic unities, he could not accept his extremely romanesque taste: his favorite work was the *Roland furieux*. Yet, he had to appear at this time to be in complete accord with him. The count of Belin, like most people interested in literature in this period, had become obsessed by the controversy over the *Cid* by Corneille. He had as a protégé, Mairet, who felt threatened by the popularity of Corneille, so that, even though he was not an ardent admirer of the unities, the count of Belin persuaded Scarron to write a pamphlet against Corneille. Here, our poet had to compromise his principles, since, as evinced in the *Roman comique* he was a fervent admirer of Pierre Corneille. In 1637 appeared the prose pamphlet *Apologie pour monsieur Mairet contre les calomnies du sieur Corneille de Rouen*. This scurrilous pamphlet was followed by a second one written in satirical verse even more violent than the first. In it he recommended that Corneille should be beaten with a club.[25]

Whatever favor Scarron expected to gain from these violent invectives was lost when the count de Belin died suddenly at the end of that year. The bishop de Beaumanoir died soon after. Thus, the author found himself without his two most powerful sponsors. He even had to find another place to live, since the new bishop was not very friendly to him.

The future looked quite bleak, his literary talents no longer
protected by the count, and his ecclesiastical career no longer
backed by the bishop. And the year 1638 was to put an end to his
third ambition: that of being the perpetual lover-hero of a Spanish
novela as well as a true *débauché:* he was besieged by a strange malady
which was gradually to paralyze him the rest of his life and would
make him suffer tremendously from that time on. There are several
accounts as to the causes of the malady. The most popular version
which places the event at the time of the Carnival of 1638 in Le Mans
seems to have been started by La Beaumelle and is not based on
historical facts, according to Chardon in *Scarron inconnu.* Here
is Naomi Phelps's account of it:

Unwilling to give up the fun he bent all his ingenuity to the problem and
evolved a disguise which he thought would be impenetrable. Stripping to
the skin, he smeared his entire body with honey; then, slashing a mattress,
rolled in the feathers, emerging an enormous, bizarre bird. Thus he went
out to join the revelers. Instantly his exotic appearance attracted a large
crowd, a circumstance which had not occurred to the wayward *abbé.* Everyone was eager to know the secret of the strange bird. A few bold ones began
to pluck the feathers. When they discovered a naked priest beneath they
were shocked at the audacity of his disguise, particularly the women, who
nevertheless plucked more assiduously than ever. In terror for his reputation, perhaps even for his life, Scarron fled through the streets followed
by the shrieking mob. Searching madly for escape he leaped over a bridge
and dived into the River Sarthe, where he remained immersed to his chin
until the crowd scattered.[26]

Tallemant des Réaux in his *Historiettes* mentions that Scarron's
illness was due to a drug administered to him by a quack doctor
to cure him from a *maladie de garçon.*[27] Naomi Phelps discusses
all the different accounts and comes to the conclusion that Scarron
suffered from multiple rheumatoid arthritis.

Scarron has written little of his reaction to the terrifying malady.
At the age of twenty-eight, a man that loved the vitality of living
had become a cripple. He needed a cane to be able to attend the
social functions at the *château* of Lavardin, the only oasis of cos-
mopolitanism remaining in the town of Le Mans. It is very difficult to determine his immediate reaction, and yet it was this
malady that eventually led him to write serious works, as he himself
states. It is possible that in the lonely and suffering days of 1638
he began to conceive of his future novel: a sensitive but frivolous

youth was again presented with the riddle of existence—he had been able to dismiss a vicious stepmother and an impotent father with burlesque. Now that life itself threatened him, how was he to react?

On December 26, 1639, Marie de Hautefort left Paris and went to live at Le Mans. Paul Scarron was one of the few people that were admitted to her intimate circle of friends. She believed her task to be to reform the *débauché* and thus helped the crippled poet react with a new seriousness to his condition. Scarron gave her his eternal adoration and admiration in a spiritual manner. This was the type of love that Marie longed for, and it certainly provided a new point of view to the frivolous *abbé*. The purity and idealism of their relationship certainly were in sharp contrast with his previous attitude toward women. According to Emile Magne, Marie de Hautefort "transformed the burlesque rhymer into a poet, stimulating in him emotion, and a thousand shades of feeling in which traces of love could be found."[28]

Marie de Hautefort, exiled by Richelieu, who thought she had too much influence on Louis XIII through her love for him, was to remain in Le Mans three years. Paul Scarron, soothed and given new hope by "Madame Sainte Hautefort"[29] and finally rewarded with a prebend, left for Paris in 1640. Again, in the life of Scarron, a bitter experience is counterbalanced by a vision of the ideal. Ugliness and beauty are fused. This dualism will be present in his masterpiece, the *Roman comique,* a work set in Le Mans and thus undoubtedly linked to his reactions to life in this town from 1633 to 1640.

V *Scarron and the Burlesque* (1640–1651)

Although a discussion of the genesis of the *Roman comique* must certainly take into account the period from 1633 to 1640, there is little evidence in the years to follow that Scarron was planning to write such a novel. The Scarron of the 1640's is not the mature author of the *Roman comique* or the *Léandre et Héro,* where the tension between the romanesque and the comical cries out for a solution. The man we are presented with in this early literature does not envision the type of love the poet felt for Marie de Hautefort. Whatever his feelings, his writings show only his bent for the burlesque. It may be said that he was writing solely to entertain, to counteract his frustration and not to express his anguish.

Unfortunately, it is this type of work that led to Scarron's great popularity during his time. This is why today readers associate Scarron with the burlesque alone. This association requires a definition of the term burlesque. For M. Victor Fournel, the burlesque genre means only a travesty: an attack on people of high station by making them speak or act basely.[30] Paul Morillot disagrees with Fournel's definition, stating that it is too narrow. He contends that the period of the Fronde in France was one in which the burlesque attained great popularity but that Fournel's definition would exclude most of the works considered burlesque by seventeenth-century opinion. He states: "What is essential is to distinguish it from the comic, which belongs to all epochs and nations. There is only a difference in degree, and not in nature, since both have as objects the creation of laughter; but the comic creates laughter only out of those things that are laughable, and the burlesque, by choice, creates laughter out of everything, particularly out of serious matters."[31]

Therefore, although Morillot tends to agree with Fournel, he tries to soften the definition by making the difference one of degree. A similar attitude is taken by Robert Berens who states: "Although the burlesque has parody-like overtones, it is not exclusively a parody or a travesty. It is language, style and temperament, and always intends to mock something that is elevated. It is more an *esprit* than a genre. Essentially, the burlesque is an attack on what is proper and seemly. It consists of a severe contrast between the subject and the way in which the subject is treated.[32]

The burlesque, then, can be considered as a particular *esprit* that existed in France at a specific historical moment. When Mazarin and other personages of high stations were being brought down by satire and ridicule through the Fronde, it is fitting that the literary inclinations of the people be toward the debasement of the newly acquired concepts of Neoclassicism. It was a passing attitude that soon degenerated and disappeared leaving the Classical tenants and the order and formalism of the court of Louis XIV victorious.

Scarron, come to Paris to make a name for himself, and acutely aware of his powers as a satirist already employed in his pamphlets against Corneille and in his early life as a reaction against his family life, realized that he could produce literature that would sell just by using this gift. Later in life, once he had become established and could write what he desired, he would voluntarily give up his role as burlesque poet and venture toward the romanesque while keeping in sight the anachronisms and ironies of actual and fictional existence. He would then create a literature where much of the burlesque would be discarded for the comical, as defined by Morillot. However the tension between the romanesque ideal and the often comical realities would at times seem to add up to a burlesque on life.

In addition to his desire to live in Paris, Paul Scarron's trip to that city in 1640 had a double purpose: first, to obtain a cure for his disease, second, to obtain a pardon for his father. The counselor had been exiled by Richelieu for resisting his will on several matters, mainly the establishment of the French Academy and the creation of sixteen new judicial posts to fill the treasury. However, soon after his arrival in Paris the poet had another attack of his illness which prevented him from acting on his father's behalf. Someone recommended to him the baths at Bourbon-l'Archambault, and he was soon on his way to try to find the needed relief.

Although the baths soothed his aching body, they did not cure him. His stay there was not wasted. As a result of his voyage to this distinguished watering place, where he met the duc de Longueville and Gaston d'Orléans, brother of the king, Scarron wrote a first, and then a second, *Légende de Bourbon,* commemorating his two trips to the baths in 1641 and 1642. These were written in the form of verse letters addressed to Marie de Hautefort. They constitute a commentary on the social life of the area and were Scarron's first long works bearing his name. The *Légendes* were soon passed around in aristocratic circles and praised. Their success led Scarron to become a professional writer. As stated before, his only purpose at this time was to gain financial success so as to be able to continue his cures.

Other early poems include the *Foire de Saint-Germain* which describes the annual fair, and the *Requeste du petit Scarron au Grand Cardinal* where he pleaded for his father, asking that he be allowed to return to Paris. He ended his poem as follows: "Done in Paris, this last day of October, by me Scarron who in spite of myself am sober, the year that the famous Perpignan was taken and, without cannon, the city of Sedan."[33] As Naomi Phelps points out, it was possibly this conclusion that turned away the cardinal's anger since Perpignan was the high point of Richelieu's campaign against Spain.[34]

The cardinal died before he could dismiss the charges against

the counselor. Scarron then turned to the king himself and wrote
a *Requeste au Roi*. The king was also in his last years of life and was
thus inclined to pardon his enemies; but when the edict was finally
passed the counselor had already died in exile.

The first year of the regency, 1643, sees the publication of Scarron's
Recueil de quelques vers burlesques. The public's response was
so laudatory that Scarron was even more encouraged to become
a professional writer. These early poems are not to be considered
burlesque in the strictest sense of the word. According to Morillot's
definition they would fall under the term comical. Thus, they were
in harmony with the times. Saint-Evremond, discussing this period
later while in exile, wrote:

> *J'ai vu le temps de la bonne régence,*
> *Temps où régnait une heureuse abondance,*
> *Temps où la ville aussi bien que la cour*
> *Ne respiraient que les jeux de l'amour.*[35]

(I have seen the times of the good regency/a time when joyous abundance
reigned/a time when town and court/breathed only love in sport.)

The *bonne régence* is to be distinguished from the latter period
when Mazarin tries to gain control of the government and rule
like another Richelieu. This is a period when freedom in love and
politics was predominant in Paris. Scarron enjoyed it and contributed to the gaiety of the *ambiance* through the agility of thought
found in his poetry where the vulgar and the noble were expressed
in the same line to provide a picturesque panorama of society.

Marie de Hautefort was back in Paris now that the king had died.
She had been recalled by the queen mother. Scarron was very
pleased to see her again, and she introduced him to many important
people at court. At this time Scarron also frequented the house of
Ninon de Lenclos and Marion de Lorme, while many visitors came
to see him, including Sarrasin, Segrais, and the Cardinal de Retz.

The *Recueil* was followed in 1644 by the publication of *Typhon,*
a truly burlesque poem which ridicules the concept of the Olympian
gods, so revered by his father's favorite poet Ronsard. By this time
all of Paris was aware of the genius of the crippled poet and wondered
at his ability to laugh in the midst of suffering. Scarron wrote his
first play at this time:[36] *Jodelet ou le maître valet* which he dedicated
to the commandeur de Souvré who had obtained for him a pension

from the queen mother. Reportedly, the play was written in three weeks. Nevertheless, it was an instant and tremendous success and marks the beginning of his career as a playwright. The times, however, were changing. One such indication is the second exile of Mme de Hautefort; this time to a convent. The queen mother was every day more and more influenced by the Italian Mazarin who was in turn hated and mocked by the people. Her passion for him was silently condemned by her favorite, Marie de Hautefort. This reminder of her own weakness could not be tolerated.

The rise of Mazarin ends the period of the *bonne régence.* His sordid avarice, his unusual manners, and his desire for power brought a hostile and mocking reaction from the people that had gotten used to these good years. The use of the burlesque parallels the rise of Mazarin, and the advent of the "comic opera war" where everything is degraded and ridiculed marks the highest peak of success of the genre. According to Antoine Adam, Scarron is the only successful burlesque poet of France in this period. Most others lack finesse, propriety, and the gift to write literature. In addition to the *Typhon,* and his minor poems published in 1643, 1647, and 1651, Scarron left us two other burlesque writings: the *Virgile travesti* begun in 1648 and the *Mazarinade* or invective against Mazarin and the role he played in the Fronde.

Neither of these works, his major contributions to the burlesque, is read or appreciated today. Thus, the term "burlesque" when applied to Scarron has little meaning in respect to our appreciation of the poet today. His attitude toward the burlesque will be discussed in the chapter dealing with his poetry. However, it should be pointed out that Scarron wrote the *Virgile travesti* only because he knew he was capable of performing this task better than anyone in Paris at the time and because he needed the money that would derive from such publications. However, with the publication of Book V in 1649 Scarron confesses he is already tired of the burlesque and condemns it in his dedication. Although he continued writing at this time, he never completed the work. Later, when the Père Vavasseur writes his *De Ludicra dictione* against the burlesque mode, Scarron states in a letter that he is not angry with the Père Vavasseur; furthermore, he affirms he understands the genre should be condemned. It is more difficult to ascribe a definite purpose to his *Mazarinade.*[37] It has little literary value and is as vicious as his letters against

Corneille. It may be that the great avarice and desire for domination of Mazarin reminded him of his stepmother. Also, his wit was so well known that many of the slanderous labels of the Fronde were aligned with his name. This caused the queen mother to suspend a pension she had granted him. Scarron, very sensitive about his financial condition, may have reacted by siding with the *frondeurs* in the "make believe" war against the crown. With the conclusion of the Fronde (1652), Scarron emerges as a serious writer with a bent for the romanesque. It is this last period of his life that produced most of the works for which he is remembered, including his masterpiece, the *Roman comique.*

VI *Scarron and the Romanesque*[38]

The change from the burlesque poet who only wrote for profit to the serious author of the 1650's was not made abruptly. Therefore, before considering this period one must look back to find traces of the new Scarron in the early period. The theater is probably a good indication of the temper of the poet. Although his first comedy was written in three weeks and is not a serious work, but one designed only to make the audience laugh, it is significant that Scarron modeled his play after a Spanish *comedia* by Agustín de Rojas. His interest in the Spanish works of the Golden Age will lead him away from the purely farcical and burlesque. He will note that the *comedia* combines serious elements with comical scenes. This he will consider an imitation of life, while the works of the Classical authors would appear artificial to the cripple. The humor in the Spanish plays was usually found in the statements made by servants. The creation of Jodelet by Scarron is significant since he is the ancestor of such servants as Mascarille and Scapin that will be found in the plays of Molière. Thus, Scarron's creation of *Jodelet ou le maître valet* points out Scarron's perception of how to establish a new type of comedy in France: his bent for the romanesque in using complex plots; and his imitation of the Spanish in the use of the serious and the comical in one work to create a unity derived from the observation of life.

This play was followed by *Les trois Dorotées ou le Jodelet souffleté,* created in the same manner as the previous comedy to profit from its success. However, it was received coldly. To this he added *Les Boutades du Capitaine Matamore* and *L'Abrégé de comédie ridicule de Matamore,* which can be included in the burlesque genre.

Scarron had in the meantime (1646) taken a six-week trip to Le Mans to protect his prebend. Being already a cripple it is very unlikely that Scarron gathered at this time much material for the composition of his *Roman comique*. It is possible, however, that the visit encouraged him to write such a novel. In fact, the first mention of this project is found two years after his return from Le Mans: Vincent Voiture had died that year, and Scarron wrote in his memory the *Relation véritable*. In the dedication addressed to Gilles Ménage and Jean François Sarrazin,[39] Paul Scarron states: "The book which I am dedicating to you contains nearly a thousand lines; each of you will then have five hundred for his share. You merit more, certainly, and I had planned to add a short novel begun some time ago, which seemed rather promising; but whether by fate or by my fault I was unable to prevent my hero's sentence to hanging at Pontoise; and that hanging is so *vraisemblable* that I feel incapable of changing the story without giving a bad turn to my novel and making an error in judgment."[40]

The roots of the *Roman comique* and of the late romanesque plays of Scarron must therefore be found in the years of the Fronde when his burlesque spirit reached a high point in the *Virgile travesti*. It is at this time that Scarron installs himself in the Hôtel de Troyes, an apartment so spacious he must yield part of it to Esprit Cabart, seigneur de Villermont. This man will be important in the life of Scarron since he influenced him in three major respects, all of which are related to the romanesque; and indeed Cabart de Villermont was a man of vast culture, whose travels and adventures in America could have filled at least one volume of La Calprenède. His role in the genesis of the *Roman comique* will be discussed in the following chapter. It should only be noted here, to show evidence of Scarron's more serious attitudes, that the poet was interested in translating the *Morale* of Gassendi, in the late 1640's. Indeed it was probably in the years 1649 to 1651 that the greatest changes occurred in Scarron. He was contemplating in the Fronde the result of the burlesque attitude toward life, a spectacle much more deplorable than the stilted attitude of the *précieuses* which he had ridiculed. According to Sainte-Beuve, "Scarron opposed all the *précieux* that surrounded him, using the burlesque as antidote."[41] Opposing the extremes of Sapho whose salon discussed the nuances of love in its purest forms and drew them in the *carte de tendre,* there was the vital laughter of the grotesque poet: this was the role which Scarron was playing.

Yet the chaos that ensued from too much downgrading of the ideal in human nature was not pleasing to Scarron either. A balance had to be attained between preciosity and the burlesque. Led by the exotic vision of Cabart de Villermont, and confronted with the Fronde, the cripple began to develop his individual attitudes oblivious of the still existing public taste for the burlesque.

Many indications exist of this change in attitude, and some have already been mentioned: his interest in the Spanish *comedia;* the statements made in 1649 condemning the burlesque in the preface to the fifth book of the *Virgile travesti;* his sudden interest in translating Gassendi, the contemporary alternative to Descartes; the appearance of several poems imitated from the Spanish in the third part of the *Oeuvres burlesques* of 1651; and finally the publication that same year of the first part of the *Roman comique.*

Agonizing over his participation in the Fronde, Scarron refused to answer Cyrano de Bergerac's brutal attacks on him and the burlesque genre. Cyrano had equated Scarron with rebellion against justice by stating: "Seditious nation, come and see a spectacle worthy of God's justice! It's the horrible Scarron, given to you as an example of the punishment suffered in Hell by all ingrates, traitors and backbiters of their sovereigns."[42] It is in these confused years that, according to Emile Magne, "Scarron slowly returned to order, preparing the appearance of the *Roman comique.*"[43] He liked to read portions of it to his friends and ask for their approval; and, when it was published, he sent copies to them asking for their reactions. It was Scarron's first adventure into prose fiction. Yet, it is a masterpiece that emerges from the chaos of the Fronde and reaches out for a new order in thought and literature.

Cabart de Villermont, in addition to guiding Scarron on his *Roman comique,* was responsible for instilling in the poet a desire to live in America, the romantic ideal of primitive nature: "I renounce burlesque verses, comical romances, and comedies in order to go to a country where false practitioners of religion, inquisitions, winters that kill, abscesses which maim me, and wars that cause me to die of hunger will not exist."[44]

Cabart de Villermont was also responsible for arranging a meeting between Scarron and Françoise d'Aubigné, a girl who was to become very important in his life. One day in the year 1650, in the midst of the Fronde, while Scarron was seated in his famous chair at the Hôtel de Troyes, he was visited by this fourteen-year-old girl, granddaughter of Théodore Agrippa d'Aubigné, equally known as soldier, novelist, historian, and poet. Her reaction on seeing the unfortunate poet was to burst into tears. This is the beginning of one of the most amazing love affairs in history, which finally ended in marriage in 1652. It should be noted that the poet at first offered Françoise to provide a dowry for her which she refused. It is then that he proposed marriage to which she readily consented. Therefore, it was certainly not out of interest, but out of genuine affection, that she married Paul Scarron. At the marriage ceremony, the secretary inquired as to the dowry of the bride. Scarron answered: "Immortality! The names of King's wives die with them; that of Scarron's wife will live eternally."[45] This remark is significant because later, after the poet's death, Madame Scarron was to become the famous Mme de Maintenon, wife and counselor of Louis XIV.

It is while he was considering his marriage with Françoise that the poet was also considering going to America. As early as 1650 he and Cabart de Villermont had become involved with the Société des Indes Equinoxiales which was planning to exploit *La Guyane*. His interest in Françoise d'Aubigné only increased his interest in America since she had lived there and Cabart de Villermont had met her in Martinique. Many of the Frenchmen of the period were considering this migration. Scarron's stated purpose was to find there a cure for his illness, but even in this, the idealized concept of America can be seen. The poet wanted to enter into a new life— to take a beautiful and sensitive girl to America was certainly a romanesque and idyllic adventure. Yet, his actions would not be interpreted by others in this light. Instead, his contemporaries, and even many critics today must relate all his actions to the burlesque. A fellow novelist, Furetière, on learning of his trip, states: "So, that famous paralytic who crawled along with many a moan, is starting on a journey to America, like Vespucci or Magellan? . . . I wish I may die if he is not setting about the most burlesque of all his works."[46]

When Scarron was finally ready to depart to America with his new wife, it was too late since the expedition had already sailed. This was fortunate for the poet and his wife since that voyage ended in disaster.

Scarron felt that he had to leave Paris, even though he could not go to America. His reason: the Fronde was over, and Mazarin

was returning to the capital, ready to avenge the insults of the *frondeurs;* and the cardinal could have hardly forgotten Scarron's
pamphlet. His stay in Touraine did not last long. Both he and
his wife enjoyed the atmosphere of the capital and were bored
by the countryside. Yet, he had managed to write: he probably
worked on the second part of the *Roman comique*[47] and revised
Dom Japhet d'Arménie. More important, he expresses his feelings
in the *Epître chagrine à Rosteau.* In it, he laments the state of literature after the death of Richelieu. Writers receive little for great
works these days, he states: witness Corneille, Tristan l'Hermite,
and the Scudérys. His *Roman comique* and *Dom Japhet* are equally
unrewarding. Notice that Scarron compares himself at this point
with the more serious authors of the time. The burlesque poet
has given way to the man who appreciates serious works and worries
about the future of such an art.

Scarron and his wife returned quietly to Paris, and in February,
1654, they were settled in a large *hôtel* on the rue Neuve Saint-Louis.
Soon all was back to normal: the publishers were demanding more
writings by Scarron,[48] while the public came to see the *malade
de la Reine* and his wife, *la jeunne Indienne:* all were curious to see
the cripple who in the midst of his pain laughed more than anyone
in Paris, accompanied by a wife considered one of the great beauties
of the time. Theirs became one of the more popular salons in Paris
now that the Hôtel de Rambouillet was closed and the Hôtel of
Mlle de Scudéry was becoming too affected and *précieux* for most.

Among the men of letters that came to the Hôtel Scarron were the
abbé de Boisrobert, Tristan l'Hermite, the rival of Corneille, the
Neoclassical critic Chapelain, the novelist La Calprenède, the painter
Pierre Mignard who did a portrait of Françoise d'Aubigné, Segrais
who left many amusing anecdotes about Scarron, and even
Madeleine de Scudéry. In *La Clélie* she includes several portraits
of the couple under the names of Scaurus and Lyriane. Sommaize
includes them also in his *Dictionnaire des précieuses* under the names
of Straton and Stratonice.

The friendship with the abbé de Boisrobert did not last long,
however; it suddenly came to an end with the question of *L'Ecolier
de Salamanque* in 1654. The facts of this case are not absolutely
clear, but it seems that Scarron, while adapting this play from
a Spanish original by Rojas, read parts of it to those assembled
at his house. This was his usual custom since he tried most of his

works on his guests before publishing them, including the *Roman comique*. Boisrobert was apparently present at one of these readings, liked the plot, and proceeded to adapt the same play. The plays were finished at the same time. Although the Hôtel de Bourgogne wanted to present Scarron's version, Boisrobert exerted pressure to have his presented through the intervention of a lady. A play by Thomas Corneille on the same subject was produced a little later. The three plays were presented then in the same year with the Bourgogne possibly alternating between two of them. When the play was published, Scarron wrote a poem bitterly condemning Boisrobert.[49] The "quarrel" did not end here and later embraced Boisrobert's brother, Antoine Le Metel, sieur d'Ouville, who accused Scarron of borrowing from María de Zayas while pretending to write original *nouvelles*. The cripple was beginning to publish in 1655 his *Nouvelles tragi-comiques*, and d'Ouville answered with *Les Nouvelles amoureuses et exemplaires*. Later in 1657 Boisrobert was to continue the quarrel with the *Nouvelles héroïques et amoureuses*.

In addition to the *Nouvelles*, Scarron was engaged in several other literary projects in 1655. Although his fame was increasing, his monetary situation was critical. With the help of Pellison he obtains a pension from Nicolas Foucquet, the *surintendant des finances*, and dedicates to him *Le Gardien de soy-même*.[50] He will later dedicate to Foucquet's wife the second part of the *Roman comique*. Scarron also presents this year *Le Marquis ridicule*, one of his most successful plays. Still lacking funds, Scarron begins the publication of a weekly *Gazette burlesque*, at the suggestion of the printer Alexandre Lesselin. According to his biographers, the reason why Scarron stopped the publication of this *gazette* before the year was over, was his failing health and lack of interest.

F. Lachèvre, in his edition of the *Gazette*, brings up a question largely ignored by biographers: Scarron's relationship to the trial of Jean l'Ange and Michel Millot over the publication of *L'Escole des filles*. He and Pierre Louÿs believe that the reason why Scarron ceased writing his *Gazette* was that he had to go into hiding because of the trial.[51] *L'Escole des filles* had been secretly printed in 1655 by Louis Piot, and indeed it could have never been authorized since it is considered the first erotic manual to be published in France. Piot, L'Ange, and Millot, to deceive the authorities, had placed the simple statement "A Leyden" instead of pub-

lisher and the actual place of publication. Thus the authorities
would not think it had been published in Paris, but in Holland.
Yet Piot, after collecting his fee, fearful of being caught, turned
L'Ange over to the authorities. The authorities never arrested Millot,
and L'Ange was freed after a token sentence. The books, however,
were recovered except eight copies which had been given to Scarron.
The authorities knew about these and never tried to retrieve them.
One of these copies Scarron gave to the *surintendant des finances,*
Foucquet, and in 1661, when he was arrested it was found in a secret
drawer. These and other facts lead Lachèvre to surmise that Scarron
had written this work. Knowing how Scarron would write almost
anything to obtain money, as evinced by his *Mazarinade* and his
pamphlets against Corneille, this becomes a plausible assumption.
There is, however, no proof that Scarron did write *L'Escole des
filles,* and it might have been a translation made by him from an
Italian source. [52]

In 1656 Scarron finished the tragicomedy of the late Tristan
l'Hermite, *Les Coups de l'amour et de la fortune,* and wrote the
famous ode *Léandre et Héro.* 1657 sees the publication of the
second part of the *Roman comique,* which is very successful. Even
Louis XIV reads it. Scarron meets Christina of Sweden, the protectress of Descartes to whom he states he would be a little Roland
if he were not so ill. This allusion to Ariosto certainly reflects his
bent for the romanesque, and indeed, the last three years of his
life are an adventure into this realm. As Lancaster points out, his
last few plays are saturated with exotic adventure and romance,
and he is still writing *nouvelles* based on Spanish material. Led
by his guides into the realm of the unknown, the Chevalier de Méré
and Cabart de Villermont, Scarron experiments with alchemy.
He dies on October 5 or 6, 1660, leaving behind many unfinished
works that testify to his final submergence into the romanesque.
His only regret in dying, he states, is not being able to leave his
wife as much as he wanted so that she could live in comfort. Scarron
wrote his own epitaph:

> *Celui qu'ici maintenant dort*
> *Fit plus de pitié que d'envie,*
> *Et souffrit mille fois la mort*
> *Avant que de perdre la vie.*
> *Passant, ne fais ici de bruit,*

Garde bien que tu ne l'éveilles;
Car voici la première nuit
Que le pauvre Scarron sommeille.[53]

(He who now sleeps here/evoked more pity than envy,/and suffered death a thousand times/before losing his life./Passerby, don't make any noise,/ be careful not to wake him;/since this is the first night/in which the poor Scarron can sleep.)

CHAPTER 2

The Roman Comique,
General Considerations

I *The French Novel in the Seventeenth Century*[1]

THE *Roman comique* of Paul Scarron is regarded by most as contributing to the literary Fronde which tried to destroy idealistic forms of fiction in this period. In order to evaluate this proposition, the history of the seventeenth-century novel should be analyzed. According to Antoine Adam, the novel of this century can be divided into four periods.[2] The earliest type was the sentimental novel. Its model can be found in Boccaccio's *Fiammetta*, translated into French in 1532. Some of its elements include: the idealization of man by woman, as told in the first person by the heroine; analysis of passion; potential adultery; and a tragic conclusion. As early as 1538 this type of fiction had entered into France: Helisenne de Crenne in the *Angoisses douloureuses* presented a similar theme which also ends tragically. With the seventeenth century, however, an important reversal occurs: it is man that idealizes and serves woman. Vital d'Audiguier presents an excellent example of this type of fiction in the *Histoire tragi-comique de nostre temps, sous les noms de Lysandre et Caliste,* written in 1615. Here, Lysandre loves Caliste who is married to Cléandre. The plot winds through many romanesque and supernatural adventures which include encounters with pirates and ghosts, secret ointments and pilgrimages, to attain in this case a happy end.[3]

Up to this point, it should be noticed, passion flows from the existence of an obstacle. Eros triumphs outside the social framework, creating an essentially destructive love.[4] However, paralleling the publication of many sentimental novels is the appearance of *L'Astrée* by Honoré d'Urfé which was to become the most perused novel in the whole century, in spite of its length. It represents the final triumph of women in the Classical age. It is not, however, a sentimental novel. Its setting is pastoral, being an imitation of

Sannazaro's *Arcadia* and Jorge de Montemayor's *La Diana.* Love is no longer a dark passion existing outside society but must be considered as an integral part of it. The novel became a manual of customs and behavior for polite society, just as the *Courtier* of Castiglione had become in Italy. Astrée, the shepherdess and heroine of the novel, can banish Céladon from her presence at any time, knowing he will obey all her commands. Woman sets the rules of behavior which become extremely refined as a reaction against the coarseness of the previous century, infected by prejudices and wars of religion. Céladon, the hero, when he is banished from her presence, does not complain. He retires to the forest where he places her portrait in an altar. Thus, while in the sentimental novels love was a passion that needed an obstacle, now it is a deliberate attempt at worship. Worship demands a very exacting ritual; and this can be regarded as the obstacle. In *L'Astrée* there are tablets dictating the twelve commandments of love. Here is the first commandment:

> *Qui veut être parfait amant,*
> *il faut qu'il aime infiniment*
> *l'extrême amour seul en est digne,*
> *aussi la médiocrité*
> *de trahison est plutôt signe*
> *que non pas de fidélité.* [5]

(Whoever would perfect lover be/must perforce love endlessly/limitless love alone should stay/while mediocrity/more often signals to betray/ than to persist in fidelity.)

By 1630 the sentimental novel had disappeared, and from 1640 to 1660 a new form flourished in France, borrowing many of the love concepts of *L'Astrée.* This is the heroic novel. [6] It is this type which must be analyzed carefully since it was the prevalent one when Scarron published his *Roman comique.*

The *Roman héroïque* popularized in the works of La Calprenède and Georges and Madeleine de Scudéry, is a compendium of many different types of fiction and ideas arising out of the contemporary social milieu. This type of novel is certainly a product of earlier novels of chivalry. Herberay des Essarts had translated from the Spanish the *Amadis de Gaula* in 1540. Ever since that time the novel had been popular in France. The *roman d'aventure,* a transitional and short-lived type which flourished in the 1630's, represents the first development of the novel of chivalry to fit the character and taste of seventeenth-century France. It is further metamorphosed into the heroical. The hero throughout these novels is the perfect prince, valiant and generous. He is always sure of his actions, and always conquers the foe. Yet, his role is relegated to servitude: Amadis must always please Oriana and perform heroic deeds to merit her. She is a cruel mistress, or the *aimable inhumaine* of Corneille: witness the episode of Peña Pobre so ably parodied by Cervantes when Don Quijote does penance in the Sierra Morena. In the heroic novel, for example, Oroondate and Cyrus are perfect lovers who must merit their cruel mistresses.

Nevertheless, it would be an oversimplification to trace the worship of women to the novels of chivalry alone, since Oriana is not inaccessible and enjoys the pleasures of carnal love. Some of the ingredients of the cult are, however, present as shown in the above paragraph. The sentimental novel should also be taken into account in any discussion of the idealization of women which occurs in the heroic novel of the seventeenth century. As stated above, the Italian type has little to do with this tradition. However, the Spanish sentimental novel, particularly the works of Diego de San Pedro may have exerted their influence in the creation of the concepts present in the heroic novel. In the *Cárcel de Amor* the hero, Leriano, dies after dissolving his mistress's letters in a glass and drinking them. She had refused to marry him in spite of all his services.

The worship of women and the subservience of man can also be traced to the Renaissance in Petrarchism, the Platonism of Ficino and of Castiglione's *Courtier* where he advises his readers to flee ugliness of vulgar love related to the senses, and understand that the love of beauty is a divine thing.[7] Cyrus must remain ever faithful to Mandane, serving her and yet never revealing his love: admiration for her divine beauty is his recompense for more than ten years.

These themes were not the sole property of fiction. The nuances of feeling, the intricacies and subtle delights of ideal love were the themes discussed in the salons which followed the dictates of d'Urfé's *L'Astrée*. These salons tried to purify the spirit of France and uplift the vision of men from sensual pleasures to the workings of the *tendre*. The best-known salons were those of Mme de Rambouillet which flowered from 1630 to the time of the Fronde,

Mme de Sablé's, and Mlle de Scudéry's. The latter was somewhat
bourgeois, and encouraged *préciosité*. A vivid description of these
gatherings is presented by the abbé Pure in his novel *La Précieuse
ou le mystère des ruelles*. It is difficult to determine the author's
attitude toward these *précieux* ladies; however, the minute description of the many types of love gives the reader a good idea of the
attitudes that existed in these gatherings.

It was in the salon of Madeleine de Scudéry that the famous
carte de tendre which was included in her novel *Clélie* was created.
This map presents the different roads love can take from its beginnings in the village of *nouvelle amitié*. Two of the ways are lined
with villages and must be traveled on foot. The third is a torrential
stream that leads directly to the village of *tendre sur inclination*.
There is great danger of overshooting this village since the currents
are treacherous, and thus ending in the *mer dangereuse* on the other
side of which are the *terres inconnues*. Thus, Madeleine de Scudéry
dismisses this *tendre* for being outside her experience. It is in fact
outside the world of the heroic novel since it demands blind passion.
The other two ways lead to the *tendre sur estime* and *tendre sur
reconnaissance*. The charting of steps represented by villages points
to the fact that love has ceased to be a passion as it was in the early
sentimental novels and has become a very deliberate mode of
worship. It is this deliberate ritual which tends to present the love
attitude as artificial in the eyes of those who are not initiated into
the life of the salons. For others, this aristocratic game became an
absorbing reality. Scarron will be aware of these possibilities in the
Roman comique. He also used the charts of love to create a *carte*
of the *Empire du burlesque*.

The tenets of Classicism were also to play an important role
in the genesis of the heroic novel. Imitation of the ancients is an
essential doctrine in this school. Tragedy and the epic are thus
regarded by the Classicists as very reputable genres, and imitations
of Seneca and Virgil were common. The novel was not highly
regarded early in the century since it lacked such a tradition. What
the authors of the heroic novel did was to attempt to link the novel
with the epic. Yet, how does one reconcile the predominance of
love in the novel with the almost sole concern with war and heroic
actions present in the epic? The answer had already been given
by Torquato Tasso in Italy: "Let it be admitted, then, that a heroic
poem can be formed with an amorous subject, such as the love of

Leander and Hero, of which Musaeus, a very ancient Greek poet, wrote, and that of Jason and Medea, of which Apollonius wrote among the Greeks and Valerius Flaccus among the Latins . . . and the loves of Theagenes and Chariclea, and of Leucippe and Clitophon which were written of in the same language by Heliodorus."[8] Notice that a novel, the *Aethiopica* of Heliodorus, is included as an epic. This mistake was perpetuated by many including Sir Philip Sidney and Julius Caesar Scaliger. Thus, another element in addition to the epic was important in the creation of the heroic novel: the Byzantine romance.

Since the epic was to serve as model for the construction of these new novels, many concepts were taken from that genre and applied to the *roman héroïque:* the unities, verisimilitude, a historical setting, beginning the story *in medias res,* and the necessity of men of high station as characters. An important document in the study of the relationship of the heroical novel with the epic is Georges de Scudéry's preface to his novel *Ibrahim.* It will be discussed in detail when Scarron's relation to the heroic novel is considered in the next chapter.

Therefore, the epic, the novel of chivalry, the sentimental novel, the Greek romance, the renaissance Platonic tradition, and the attitude of the *précieuses* went into the makeup of this new type. The length of such compendiums was necessarily staggering. *Cléopâtre* by La Calprenède, for example, was divided into twelve volumes, twenty-four books, and contained a total of 4,153 pages. Yet readers avidly awaited the publication of the next volume and eagerly discussed them at the salons.

Before turning to the tradition of the comical, a few words should be said about the developments in ideal fiction during the rest of the seventeenth century. The inordinate influence of these salons on the novels led to their downfall. With *Le Grand Cyrus* by Scudéry, but mainly with *La Clélie* (1654–60), these novels lost the romanesque adventures to indulge in portraits. Important people of the time were thus depicted, and the chief aim of the readers who now bought them was to discover who was described and how.[9]

A new type of fiction began to be widely read. Its length, never more than one hundred pages, sharply contrasted with the inordinate length of the *héroïque.* This type was in imitation of the Spanish *novela.* In 1656 Segrais had published the *Nouvelles Françaises,* which, according to Dorothy Dallas, "served as transition between the novels of ten volumes and the shorter forms of fiction which made possible the creation of *La Princesse de Clèves*."[10] From this point to the end of the century, the *roman historique* reigned. The *cadre,* as in the heroic novel, is still historical, but history is taken with more seriousness, and the action is more recent. They soon were named *secret histories* and included a recent political intrigue tied to a romantic intrigue. Only three authors were successful in this form: Madame de La Fayette, the abbé de Saint-Réal, and Madame de Villedieu. Of all the novels mentioned above it is only Mme de La Fayette's *Princesse de Clèves* which holds our interest to this day.

II *The Tradition of the Comical in Fiction: Charles Sorel*[11]

During the sixteenth and seventeenth centuries, the idealized novel is paralleled by what might be called the comical in prose fiction; such is the tradition in which Scarron is placed by most critics. This tradition had as its greatest exponent in the sixteenth century, François Rabelais, whose *Gargantua* and *Pantagruel* paralleled and parodied the giants of the chivalric romances and other chronicles of the time. Yet, it is difficult to place this masterpiece in the tradition of the novel, although it certainly figures among the forerunners of this genre. George Saintsbury states in this respect: "The absence of any real plot has been sufficiently commented on, with the temptations conferred by it to substitute a fancied unity of purpose . . . the character-links are hardly stronger, . . . the scene is only in one or two chapters nominally placed in Nowhere; but as a whole it is Nowhere Else, or rather a bewildering mixture of topical assignments in a very small part of France, and allegorical or fantastic descriptions of a multitude of Utopias."[12]

In fact, the tradition of the comical during the sixteenth century is represented mainly by *conteurs.* Men like Nicolas de Troyes, Bonaventure Despériers, and Guillaume Bouchet borrow from the Italian *novelle* and from the medieval *fabliaux* to create anecdotal tales which depict the life of the common people and whose main purpose is to entertain, mainly through humor. With the seventeenth century the tradition of the *conte* gradually disappears, and in its place, the comical romances appear. These works, however, represent a very small part of the total output of fiction in the Classical age. Nevertheless, readers today consider this minor tradition more readable than the prevalent platonizing and romanesque fiction, totally divorced from the realities of the time. Some early exponents of this tradition are mentioned by Fournel.[13] They include Agrippa d'Aubigné's *Baron de Faeneste* and John Barclay's *Satires d'Euphormion*. These works have as their aim to satirize contemporary manners and customs.

Yet, it is with Charles Sorel that the comical romances of the seventeenth century fully develop: he will, then, be the main figure discussed in this section. With him three distinct types emerge, which will interact throughout the century. Thus, in stating that a particular comical romance belongs to a certain type, this will refer only to a greater reliance on a technique and must not be understood as excluding the other tendencies. The technique of parody or burlesque of idealistic forms of fiction is prevalent in the first type. It is this type which is considered typical of the comical romances and yet it accounts for only a small portion. Parody belongs to the "Fronde littéraire" that tried to destroy the conventional idealistic fiction of d'Urfé and Mlle de Scudéry. Charles Sorel's contribution to this mode is his *Berger extravagant* written in 1627 as a burlesque of the *Astrée*. At the outset of the novel, a shepherd, Lysis, tending his sheep next to a river and singing of his love for Charite reminds the reader of Céladon. However, it is soon made clear that the river is not the Lignon, but the Seine, and that we are not in the fifth century but in the times of Louis XIII. The shepherd happens to be a student who, having read the *Astrée,* has become a Don Quijote of the pastoral; the unapproachable and supreme goddess whom he worships is none other than a country wench, a servant called Catherine. The antihero is born. The burlesque has been created, and the revolution begins. This form was continued for example in Gilbert Saulnier, sieur du Verdier's *Le Chevalier hypocondriaque* (1632), and in Louis Moreau, sieur du Bail's *Le Gascon extravagant* (1637).

The second type comes closer to the definition previously given of the word comical; here we laugh at what is laughable: at those customs of the time which may be regarded as ironic or absurd. Thus, this second type is mainly concerned with the satire of seventeenth-century manners, although some of the works only depict such customs and condemn them through moralization and not satire. *La Vray histoire comique du Francion* is Charles Sorel's contribution to this type. Its structure resembles the work of Rabelais and the Spanish picaresque; yet there are essential differences that point to the development of the novel. In Antoine Adam's words: "It is true that one finds here multiple adventures. But, the episodes are not presented only as successive episodes. The strong personality of the hero, the existence of several figures who although definitely secondary, are still important and reappear throughout the novel with definite traits, suffice to create a unity in Sorel's novel which is not to be found in the Spanish works of this type."[14]

Sorel in *Francion* presents a comical and satirical picture of a cross-section of French society. To accomplish this he brings in not only his own personal observations of the manners of the time, but a conglomerate of literary sources. He turns to several picaresque novels for certain episodes: to Carlos Garcia's *Desordenada Codicia,* to Quevedo's *Buscón,* to Espinel's *Marcos de Obregón,* and others. French and Italian *conteurs* are also significant in the genesis of this work: Boccaccio's stories and Noël de Fail's hero, Eutrapel, are incorporated in the *Francion.* Sorel even uses passages from previous comical romances. Barclay's *Euphormio* may have not only provided Sorel with some scenes of the life at the college but may also have inspired his creation of Hortensius, the pedant schoolmaster. Contemporary anecdotes also have gone into the formulation of *Francion:* Antoine Adam points to several similarities between different episodes in Sorel's novel and anecdotes contained in the *Historiettes* of Tallemant des Réaux.

This vast *cadre* of reality and humor, a conglomerate of many traditions fused by the hope of improving mankind through generosity,[15] was published in 1623. What is significant about this date is that the previous year Sorel had published *Le Palais d'Angélie,* a novel in the romanesque tradition: one of the great comical romances was probably conceived while its author was still working on an idealistic and Platonic novel. Thus, in a discussion of Scarron, the reader should not be astonished to find the combination of both trends.

Later in life, after experimenting with other genres, Sorel returns to the comical technique in *Polyandre* (1648), where he again portrays and satirizes many types of people: the financier, the supposedly mundane and sophisticated ladies, the falsely devout women, and many others; however, this novel lacks the dynamism of *Francion.*

A third type, which employs the allegorical technique need not detain us long, since it has little bearing on Scarron. Sorel's *Relation de ce qui s'est passé en Royaume de Sophie depuis les troubles excités par la Rhétorique et l'Eloquence* (1659), is somewhat removed from the novelistic genre. It was written in reply to Furetière's *Nouvelle allégorique ou histoire des derniers troubles arrivés au royaume d'éloquence* (1656); it discusses in allegorical form literary controversies of the time and includes a description of the French Academy. This form is linked to the idealistic novel in its concern for maps. The *carte de tendre* of Mlle de Scudéry uses the same technique as a map included in Furetière's work. Sorel also composed the *Nouvelles Françaises,* adapting the Spanish *novela* to French tastes. These are longer than the anecdotal *contes* of the sixteenth century but definitely shorter than any of the heroical romances. This type of fiction has been discussed already under the heading of romanesque fiction. However, it is mentioned here because this type was essential in the disappearance of the *roman héroïque* and the creation of *La Princesse de Clèves.*

The works of Charles Sorel, then, give us a picture of the different types of comical romances that developed in France during the seventeenth century. Other than Scarron, he is considered by critics as its greatest exponent. Yet, no discussion of the comical romance would be complete without the mention of Furetière's *Roman bourgeois.* This work, written after Scarron's *Roman comique,* has been placed in the tradition of parody, since it uses a method similar to Sorel's *Berger extravagant,* a method popularized by Cervantes. The heroine, Javotte, a middle-class girl living in Paris, is introduced to the salons where the reading of *Astrée* triggers a madness very similar to that of Don Quijote and Lysis. In trying to act as a *précieuse* and a heroine of romances, she parodies the type of fiction she imitates and that is read at the salons, since their complete irrelevance to the realities of the world becomes apparent.

Although the *Roman bourgeois* can be considered as a parody of the heroical novel, many of its elements cannot be reduced to this function. The description of the middle-class milieu, centering in the *Place Maubert*; the hopes and fears of Vollichon, father of Javotte; Lucrèce's concern with marriage; and the avarice of Jean Bedaut certainly enlarge the scope of the novel to include a *peinture de la société bourgeoise.* This description of bourgeois manners is not presented objectively, since the author emphasizes the pettiness of their concerns. Furetière does not offer imitation of the aristocracy as a substitute: it has been pointed out that Javotte's acceptance of the aristocratic vision serves the author to parody heroical romances. No solution is offered. Yet, one element present in this radical satire leads us to a panorama of fiction in this century: the author's aristocratic point of view.

In general, that which distinguishes the Classical novel from later forms is the author's relationship to the aristocracy. A man of letters at this time has to have a Maecenas (Scarron called himself the "Queen's invalid," and it has been shown how he changed some of his views to please some of his protectors), while he and his works are to be exhibited at the aristocratic salons. This close relationship between the author and a particular class often leads him to view the world from their perspective.

As the seventeenth century progressed, the movement toward the purification of French language and manners began to be imitated by the bourgeois and the people from the provinces. Comparing the years before and after 1650, Antoine Adam states: "The *Hôtel de Rambouillet* was open only to an aristocratic élite and to several brilliant minds invited for their pleasant company. The Saturday gatherings were reserved, however, for the middle class."[16]

Adam then states emphatically that the Saturday gatherings of Sapho (Mlle de Scudéry) are to be considered bourgeois, as opposed to the early aristocratic gatherings of Mme de Rambouillet which ended at the time of the Fronde. Such an intrusion by bourgeois and provincials in what was considered fashionable caused strong reactions. The upper class believed that these people, lacking poise and self-control, carried the movement to an extreme: the simple principles of gallantry and *honnêteté* were carried to the extreme of *préciosité;* in the bourgeois salons countless rules of behavior were created which had to be followed. These rules progressively became more and more divorced from society. Language followed suit. More important, the aristocracy had regarded, for example, the twelve tablets containing laws for becoming a perfect lover, as an attempt to provide them with *manuels de civilité;* in other words, these were games which were to be played: their role was to be ideal courtiers. Even if their character prevented them from such actual behavior, they must maintain the *appearance*. This last word was

the key to their behavior. The bourgeois, on the other hand, could
not distinguish between role and character. As they began reading
these works they longed to become an ideal man or woman without
regard to their frailties or shortcomings. Becoming convinced they
had achieved their goal, many paraded their newly acquired sensibilities only to be scorned by connoisseurs of the game.

It is this situation which led to the composition of many comical
romances and comedies at this time. In the theater, Molière is
a clear exponent of the aristocratic viewpoint in *Les Précieuses
ridicules* and *Le Bourgeois gentilhomme.* In the novel, the same can
be said of Sorel's *Berger extravagant,* where idyllic love of two com-
moners is satirized. A similar viewpoint is found in the *Roman
bourgeois* of Furetière, as stated above, and this will certainly be
true also of the *Roman comique* where the character of Ragotin,
a man of the provinces and a bourgeois with aristocratic pretensions,
is satirized by Scarron. Thus, this aristocratic attitude created by
the extremes to which some provincials and bourgeois carried their
affectations will be an essential consideration in many novels of this
period and must be taken into account in a discussion of the *Roman
comique.*

III *The Plot of the* Roman comique

Before proceeding with a discussion of the *Roman comique*
a brief summary of the plot will be given to facilitate reference.
The novel deals with the trials and tribulations of a troupe of actors
that wander through the French countryside. The first few lines
are often quoted: "Bright Phoebus had already performed above
half his career; and his chariot having passed the meridian, and got
on the declivity of the sky, rolled on swifter than he desired. Had
his horses been willing to have made use of the slopingness of the
way, they might have finished the remainder of the day in less than
half a quarter of an hour; but instead of pulling a main, they curveted
about snuffing a briny air, which set them aneighing, and made
them sensible that they were near the sea, where their father is said
to take his rest every night. To speak more like a man, it was five
or six of the clock, when a cart came into the market place of
Mans."[17]

Indeed, throughout the work, the author will use a very direct
and clear style, interrupting the narrative to add personal comments
and humorous asides. This familiar style is a reaction to the *précieux*

style of the heroical novels. This style will sometimes blend with
the subject matter, particularly when dealing with the adventures
of Ragotin. On other occasions it will clash with the serious topic
being discussed, thus creating a burlesque atmosphere. However,
there are many instances when the author is serious about a serious
subject matter, as in the *récits* of Destin and La Caverne. Here,
the romanesque tendencies of the author emerge the clearest. These
changes of tone should be kept in mind; otherwise, any analysis
of the action would be meaningless.

The cart drawn by oxen which entered the town of Le Mans
carried three actors—Destin, La Caverne, and La Rancune.
Although part of their troupe is missing, they are persuaded to
present a play that night near the Inn of La Biche which will be
their home in Le Mans. The play is never concluded since a fight
breaks out. That evening La Rappinière, the provost of the town,
asks the actors to spend their first night at his house. This serves
to focus on the character of the law officer, who turns out to be
extremely vain and of a very suspicious and avaricious nature. The
actors are finally reunited and the reader is introduced to Estoile,
Olive, Léandre, Angélique, and Roquebrune. In addition, he is
introduced to a little lawyer, "the greatest little fool that ever ran
madding about since Orlando Furioso,"[18] who wants to join the
troupe. He is named Ragotin. This lawyer tells a short story, the
tale of "The Invisible Mistress." Up to this point the author has
mainly dealt with character, making apparent some of the shortcomings of La Rappinière and La Rancune, while Destin, Estoile,
Léandre, and Angélique are praised and almost idealized. Some
incidents, in particular the strange behavior of Doguin, valet of
La Rappinière, point to mysteries not solved and thus create some
suspense. Other incidents, like the fight after the play, are purely
humorous. Thus, already in the first few chapters there is a mixture
of the purely comical and the romanesque.

The "History of the Invisible Mistress" is certainly a very romanesque tale in appearance. A veiled woman meets Dom
Carlos at church. They keep several rendezvous where she refuses
to remove her veil and let him see her. Even though he has never
really seen her, Dom Carlos falls in love and remains faithful to
his invisible mistress. One day, on his way to see her, the hero is
kidnapped and taken to a beautiful palace where Princess Porcia
tries to persuade him to renounce his invisible mistress by offering

the joys of the palace and her irresistible beauty in exchange. Dom
Carlos rejects her, but princess Porcia discloses herself as the invisible lady. The kidnapping had been ordered to test his faithfulness.
They are happily married. Although Ragotin claims that he wrote
the tale, a little book is discovered which contains the story.

Trying to become a part of the troupe, Ragotin takes La Rancune
to supper. He then proceeds to tell him he loves one of the actresses;
at the time, he is not sure which one he loves, although he may have
shown some inclination for Angélique; La Rancune persuades him
to love Estoile. Other humorous events take place at the inn, usually
involving Ragotin who constantly shows his shortcomings when he
is trying to impress the actors. However, disturbing events keep
occurring such as the kidnapping of the priest of Domfort, which
maintain the suspense.

Destin is persuaded to tell his story which is interspersed among
several episodes and the kidnapping of the priest. It is a long *récit*
in which, according to Antoine Adam, "One can guess at a child
substitution"[19] as in the heroic and Byzantine novels. In this story
lies the key to many of the strange occurrences that take place
throughout the novel. The deciphering of its mysteries would give
us a glimpse at the denouement of the novel.

Destin thinks of himself as the son of a small-town bourgeois.
However, his parents raised him together with a certain comte
des Glaris, and a substitution may have taken place here. Destin
studied with the sons of the baron d'Arques, a nobleman who
lived in the town. These sons were named Sainct-Far and Verville;
their characters are diametrically opposed. Destin became a very
close friend of Verville while only animosity existed between him
and Sainct-Far, a treacherous youth. The baron grew fond of our
hero and sent him with his sons to the academy and later to Italy
where they were to join an army.

Unfortunately, Destin became ill in Rome, so the two brothers
had to leave him there and go do battle with the Turks. When he
recovers he saves a young lady named Léonore from two men who
were trying to force her to unveil. His love for her is so strong that
he states: "Léonore appeared in my imagination even more beautiful
than she appeared to my sight."[20] The mysterious men fight Destin,
he is wounded, and almost dies. His bravery prompts Léonore's
mother, Mlle de la Boissière, to regard him favorably and to tell
him that a clandestine marriage had brought Léonore to the world:
the husband, however, had to go back to France and had given her

a well-furnished apartment and an adequate income. The love affair between Destin and Léonore progresses until Sainct-Far, having returned from battle, tells Mlle de la Boissière that Destin is his servant, not just a friend. Destin, disappointed, goes to war and tries to get killed but, as he states: "Fortune was as contrary in this design of mine as she had been previously."[21]

Having returned to Paris after the war, Verville, in love with Mlle de Saldagne, takes Destin into his confidence. Many romanesque adventures take place, including Mlle de Léry's disguise as a servant, duels in the night where brother has to fight brother, abductions, and recognitions. The end result is that Destin leaves the service of Verville who marries Mlle de Saldagne, while the unhappy Mlle de Léry has to marry Sainct-Far. Destin had also discovered that Saldagne, the brother of Mlle de Saldagne, is one of the mysterious assailants from Italy.

Having decided to go back to Italy and the wars, Destin encounters Léonore and her mother, who were going to Paris to be reunited with the mysterious gentleman. Their servants, however, had robbed them. Then, news had come that Léonore's father had been exiled from Paris and had gone to Holland. Returning to Paris in the company of Destin and with the aid of his money, they meet La Rancune, who offers to take them to Holland with an actor's passport. New adventures occur in Paris when they meet Saldagne and later when Destin is robbed by a mysterious assailant. It will be disclosed much later that the thief was La Rappinière, a dispenser of justice in Le Mans. When the trio arrives in Holland, they discover the gentleman has left that country for England to help the king, who is opposing the Parlement. Léonore's mother dies of frustration and Destin is robbed again. The only recourse the young lovers have is to become actors in La Rancune's troupe, pretending to be brother and sister. It is at this point that the hero takes the name of Destin, while Léonore changes hers to Estoile.

Returning to the present action after Destin's *récit,* it is discovered that love, not content with ruling the lives of Destin and Estoile, and with having caused the Trojan War, or with taking Ragotin's hunger away, also takes hold of La Rappinière, who desires Estoile after seeing her perform Ximène. Roquebrune, the troupe's poet, falls in love also. The object of his desire is Inezilla, a Spanish lady who is married to an Italian *opérateur.* La Rancune falls in love with her also.

Since vanity is one of the main traits of Ragotin, he tries to show his knowledge of horses by attempting to ride next to a carriage which is to take the troupe to a nobleman's house to perform a play. Ragotin is thrown off the horse while Scarron, using his burlesque vein, compares Ragotin to Phaëton who was thrown from his celestial ride. Ragotin is allowed to ride in the carriage, and the poet, Roquebrune, is given the horse only to be thrown also.

Having arrived at their destination, Inezilla tells a tale, "A trompeur, trompeur et demi": A young lady of model virtue who resides outside of Toledo and who is named Victoria allows herself to be seduced by Dom Antoine de Ribera after he has promised to marry her. Finding out his deception, she disguises herself and goes to Madrid where, after many intricate adventures, she finds him and marries him.

As the troupe prepares to present a play, La Caverne rushes in, stating that someone has kidnapped her daughter Angélique. She suspects Léandre. In this discordant note, the first part of the *Roman comique* ends. The second part, which appeared six years later, commences when the players rush out in search of the kidnappers. The static plot, which relied mainly on flashbacks and anecdotal tales to portray character becomes dynamic now, as the players set out to obtain justice. The tone, however, still alternates between serious and comical, since La Rancune, for example, steals a pair of boots on his way to find the kidnappers while Destin rides with a naked madman through the forest.

As the actors race through the countryside looking for the kidnappers of Angélique, her mother, La Caverne, tells Estoile the tale of her life and adventures. This story includes the dramatic episode of the murder of her mother's husband by a valet of an eminent and cruel lord, the baron de Sigognac, who later fell madly in love with La Caverne's mother.

Destin, meanwhile, finds Léandre at an inn dressed as a gentleman. He explains that he was also trying to capture the kidnappers of Angélique, and proceeds with a *récit* of his past life, which is almost as amazing as that of Destin or La Caverne. He was the son of a gentleman, but on seeing Angélique perform at La Flèche, the academy he was attending, he expressed his love for her, and joined the troupe disguised as a valet.

The tale contrasts with the arrival of Ragotin, La Rancune, and Olive at the inn, with the usual humorous adventures. La Rancune has become an expert at tricking Ragotin: the little lawyer is convinced that he has slept with the corpse of La Rancune and also that he has a dreadful disease, characterized by tremendous swellings. Madame Bouvillon, in the meantime, has been laying down elaborate plans to seduce Destin, the perfect lover, who is saved only by Ragotin's impulsiveness.

The reader then learns that another arrival is expected at this little country inn: Angélique has been released by her captors. She tells how the kidnappers had apparently mistaken her for Estoile, who is now in their power. Destin's distress is alleviated only when Garouffière, who is also in town accompanying a recently married couple and their relative Mme Bouvillon, tells him Verville, Destin's best friend, is in the neighborhood.

Verville discovers that Saldagne, the villain who is always pursuing Estoile, is the one who kidnapped her. An ingenious method is devised for her release in which Destin performs heroic deeds. It is soon discovered, however, that another attempt at *enlèvement* has occurred: La Rappinière had tried to kidnap Estoile also. Garouffière, the dispenser of justice, sends men to arrest him. While he waits, he tells a tale.

"Le Juge de sa propre cause" is a Moorish story, the most romanesque in style as well as in action. Dom Carlos and Sophie love each other and expect to be married. But Sophie is kidnapped by the Moors and taken to captivity in Africa. However, the virtuous prince of Fez, falling in love with her and knowing her heart belongs to another, generously releases her. Dressed as a man, she fights for the Spanish and earns the title of viceroy of Valencia. She then becomes dispenser of justice (like Garouffière in the main narrative). One day, Dom Carlos is brought to her, accused of kidnapping a girl named Sophie. The Viceroy reveals herself to the astonishment of the town, dispenses justice, and marries Dom Carlos.

La Rappinière is finally brought in, made to confess his attempt at kidnapping, and severely admonished. To everyone's surprise (except Destin's, who was already aware of the crime through different clues presented in the novel, mainly his conversation with Doguin), La Rappinière also confesses possession of a jewel which contains a portrait of Estoile's father, thus providing a means for future recognition as customary in Byzantine novels, a method found even in *Astrée*.

Destin and Estoile, Léandre and Angélique, again called perfect lovers by the author, and the rest of the troupe, return to Le Mans where, with the subsidy of the marquis d'Orsay, a "Modern Maecenas,"[22] the players are able to produce other *comedias.* The first to be performed is *Dom Japhet d'Arménie,* Scarron's own play which is disrupted by the foolishness of Ragotin. The second day, *Nicomède* of Corneille is presented. This presentation was not disrupted since Ragotin was not present: he had spent the afternoon with Ferdinando Ferdinandi, the husband of Inezilla, since La Rancune had persuaded him that Ferdinando was a magician and would help him in his passion for Estoile.

That night, Inezilla tells a tale: "Les Deux frères rivaux." This long interpolation deals with the love of Dom Sanche for Dorotée. Dom Sanche, however, kills Dom Diegue, his rival, to Dorotée's dismay, and has to leave town. In the meantime, Dom Juan, Dom Sanche's brother who has just arrived from the New World, begins courting Dorotée, but he is loved by her sister Feliciane. Meanwhile, Dom Sanche, after many adventures, has returned disguised as a valet. After a very confusing night, the father of the two sisters gives his consent to a marriage between Dorotée and Dom Sanche, and Feliciane and Dom Juan. The author adds: "Everything succeeded so well, that there was no disagreement between either of the parties for a long while after, which you must confess is not a little to be wondered at."[23]

While Inezilla recounted her story, it is important to note that Ragotin had fallen asleep. A goat that roamed loose at the inn, seeing Ragotin's head bouncing up and down as he slept, thought the little lawyer was wanting to play, and rammed him. On this note, the second volume ends. The conclusion was to be found in the third part which never appeared, although it is known that Scarron was working on it at the time of his death. Several *suites* of the novel will be discussed in a separate chapter.

IV   *Sources of the* Roman comique: *Observation of Life*

The people of Le Mans, proud that their city had become so famous through Scarron's novel, immediately set out to discover who among them were depicted in the *Roman comique.* Voyagers to the provincial capital were shown a portrait of Mme de Bouvillon and were led to many houses where people claimed to be descendants of the famous little lawyer, Ragotin. This should not amaze anyone. It is natural for people, particularly those who know an author, to look for themselves in a literary work. This tendency was further encouraged in the seventeenth century by the many portraits included in the heroical romances. As soon as a novel appeared, the people of the salons immediately set out to discover the *clef* or key of such a work. It should be recalled that Mlle de Scudéry included Scarron's portrait in *La Clélie,* where she named him Scaurus. According to Chardon, Philippides is another name given to the comical author in another romance.[24]

Portraits of contemporary individuals were then to be expected in the novels of the time. However, Scarron, it should be remembered, objected to many of the irrelevancies of heroic romances; for example, their style and the long digressions which changed them from fictional works to manuals of courtesy. It is possible that Scarron also objected to excessive use of portraits. Critics, however, have incessantly searched for such keys. Henri Chardon has devoted two books to this subject;[25] before him, much discussion already existed, as shown by two keys which Chardon mentions and disproves. There was also speculation that the troupe described in the *Roman comique* was that of Molière. Chardon again rejects this idea.

Chardon then proceeds to give us his own key to the novel and does produce an interesting history of many of the people living in Le Mans during the time Scarron lived there. He believes, for example, that Ragotin was actually Ambrois Denisot (other members of the same family had been previously proposed including René and Julien Denisot). Indeed, this man was living at the time Scarron stayed in Le Mans. He was a lawyer, like Ragotin, and he was also widowed. Denisot served as secretary to the bishop of Le Mans which indicates that Scarron knew him. He also wrote some Latin verse and became a priest in 1641, just as Ragotin had threatened to become. However, no physical description of this man exists, and he was not hanged, as the "hero" of Scarron's novel would be. Thus, no sure proof exists for the assertion that Ragotin is a portrait of Ambrois Denisot.

Chardon identifies the troupe as that of Filandre, which indeed performed in Le Mans at this time. Filandre's name was J.B. Mouchaingre, and he joined the troupe for the love of Angélique Moulmier. It is possible, then, that Filandre is portrayed as Léandre, who loves an Angélique. Again, these parallels offer little proof and must remain interesting hypotheses. Other character identifications like that of La Rappinière who represents François Nourry, sieur de Vauseillon; and Garouffière who represents Jacques Chouet, sieur de la Gandie, rest on even less firm grounds. Thus, as Antoine Adam states: "A single character can be identified with certainty. The marquis d'Orsay is a rendering of the count of Belin, so much involved in the birth of our Classical theater. But this 'real' person plays no role in the novel."[26]

The inclusion of a portrait of the count de Belin in the novel does not imply there must exist other portraits. It should be recalled that this man was the patron of Scarron while he was in Le Mans, and it was because of him that he wrote an invective against Corneille, a man he admired. It is possible then that in honor of this man Scarron included his portrait in the novel, a practice he may have regarded as ridiculous as the *précieux* style. This certainly does not mean that Scarron was not observant while at Le Mans. His impressions of the city and the inhabitants are very well reconstructed in the novel. In this sense, his novel is realistic. Many of the physical aspects of the city and the countryside were incorporated in the novel. For example, the Inn of La Biche actually existed, and was very near a *jeu de pomme,* as shown by Chardon.[27] But Scarron, in the composition of the novel, was not trying to present a history of the town, only his impressions of its culture and manners. Some of his characters, as will be shown later, originated from a purely literary approach, and they serve to present many of Scarron's ideas and views of the world, not just to reproduce historically, villagers of his acquaintance.

V *Alleged Spanish Sources of the* Roman comique

Many critics, aware of the great influence Spain had on Scarron's theater, have delved into the literature of that nation in order to discover a single work that may have given Scarron the idea for his *Roman comique.* Several have been suggested. These works will now be discussed to determine their significance or lack of importance in the genesis of this novel.

French translations of Spanish picaresque novels go back to 1561, with the translation of the *Lazarillo de Tormes* by Paul Baudoin. However, it is only with the seventeenth century that the popularity of the picaresque is firmly established in France. Mateo Alemán's *Guzmán Alfarache,* Espinel's *Marcos Obregón,* Quevedo's *Buscón,* and others were translated and printed with frequency during the Classical age. Scarron, who had a vast knowledge of Spanish literature, had certainly read some of these works. Critics point to the episodic adventures in the *Roman comique* and state these novels may have influenced Scarron in the structure of his work. Looking for more specific matter than just the influence of a genre, critics have discussed the possible influence of Quevedo's *Buscón* on Scarron. G. Reynier, having studied this relationship, concludes: "It does not seem that he borrowed anything from the adventurer Buscón of Quevedo, who introduces us, with Don Pablo, to a company of provincial actors."[28]

The *Lazarillo de Tormes* has also been suggested as a specific picaresque source for Scarron's novel. The poet was definitely aware of this work since he signs a letter "Lazarillo de Tormes."[29] However, no parallels have been found between the two works. Thus, Reynier points out that the genre as a whole was more impor tant in the genesis of the *Roman comique* than any specific picaresque novel; he asks: "Doesn't the hazardous life of wandering comedians offer some resemblances to the odysseys of the Spanish vagabonds?"[30] Parallels between the wandering troupe and *pícaros* do exist, mainly their incessant search for masters or patrons as the case may be. It would be just as valid, however, to assume that the episodic structure stems from the exigencies of a plot dealing with a wandering troupe which must by its very nature search for new environments to make a living. Thus, although there may be parallels between the picaresque and Scarron's novel, they are not necessarily related in such a way as to denote influence. Furthermore, as will be discussed later, Scarron tries to reduce to a minimum the episodic nature of his plot.

More important perhaps is the *Viaje entretenido* by Agustín de Rojas. Adolphe de Puibusque in the *Histoire comparée des littératures espagnole et française,* states that Scarron was inspired by this Spanish work.[31] In favor of this hypothesis, it should be noted that Scarron's first play, *Jodelet ou le maître valet,* is also based on a work by Rojas. Recalling the success of this comedy, Scarron may have used another one of Rojas' works as a source for his first novel. Reynier rejects this idea and points out that the Spanish work is not a novel but just "a fragment of the *Mémoires* of a wandering actor."[32] This is not an accurate statement. Although many autobiographical events are included, the work as a whole is fictional. It even contains an interpolated and romanesque tale dealing with the loves of Leandro and Camila. It is then quite possible that Scarron may have thought of writing about a wandering troupe when he read Rojas' work. Justo García Morales in his prologue to the Spanish work states his conviction that "It is not to be doubted that Scarron had very much in mind the work of Austín de Rojas y Villandrado in the composition of the *Roman comique*."[33] However, there are no parallels between any specific events in these works.[34]

More important than the *Viaje entretenido* in the genesis of the *Roman comique* is Miguel de Cervantes' *Don Quijote de la Mancha*. This masterpiece, as has been mentioned, became very popular in France during the seventeenth century and was the model for Sorel's *Berger extravagant*. Critics have discovered that many comical chapter headings in the *Quijote* resemble closely other such headings in Scarron's novel. Maurice Bardon finds a more important similarity in his analysis of the influence of the *Quijote* in France: "Scarron pursues in the *Roman comique* this campaign for good taste and common sense which the great Spaniard waged at the beginning of the century and which he had already inaugurated."[35]

Bardon also states that just as Cervantes approves of some novels of chivalry like the *Amadís de Gaula* which he considers a classic, so does Scarron approve of some French novels like *Astrée*. He then adds: "*Don Quijote* suggested to Scarron the idea to vary his work by mixing several *novelas* and, in fact, he interpolated in the plot of his novel four rather short tales drawn from Spanish sources and adapted to French taste."[36]

If Cabart de Villermont's testimony is added to these parallels, it becomes evident that Scarron relied heavily on *Don Quijote* in the composition of his novel. Thus, in the next chapter, when the genesis and structure of the novel are discussed, the work of Cervantes in its relationship to the *Roman comique* will be analyzed, while other Spanish works here mentioned will be neglected: even the importance of the *Viaje entretenido* can be doubted, if Scarron's interest in the theater is recalled. Specific instances of imitation from the Spanish, that is, the four interpolated stories and the source for Part I, Chapter XV will also be discussed in the next chapter.

VI *Critical Approaches: Disorder and Realism*

Before proceeding to the next chapter, a brief sketch of the history of criticism of the *Roman comique* will be presented. The ideas repeated by many critics in the last three centuries will be in sharp contrast to the approach taken in the next chapter. To the seventeenth century, Scarron was synonymous with the burlesque: Père Vavasseur's invective against the burlesque, and Scarron's surprising approval of it has already been mentioned. Only four years after Scarron's death, Charles Sorel, the most representative comical novelist of the century, wrote a work in which he discusses French literature. It is called *La Bibliothèque Françoise*. Probe fiction is divided into *romans héroïques* and *romans comiques*. Scarron is, of course, discussed in the latter section. Sorel states: "The comical story of M. Scarron describes with incomparable *naïveté* the life of several comedians and other people of all classes who entertain various and amusing adventures. It is written in a style peculiar to the author which is to mock everything—even in the narration where he himself speaks. This is really burlesque rather than comic style. Otherwise, all the parts which make up the novel, being quite diverse, one has difficulty in judging its order or its linkage as well as its main theme because it is not finished."³⁷

The main outline of Scarron criticism, particularly regarding the *Roman comique,* is already present in its totality in this paragraph: Sorel considers the novel a burlesque work and doubts there is any form of unity in the novel, since it appears to incorporate such different types of people and adventures.

Nicolas Boileau, the famous Neoclassical critic, wrote a work against the heroical novels, entitled *Les Héros de roman*. In it, Scarron, sitting by the side of Pluto, unmasks the heroes of Scudéry, La Calprenède and others, exposing them for what they really are. The name Scarron was deleted from the dialogue in 1710 when Boileau was preparing the dialogue for the press since at that time Mme Scarron, now Madame de Maintenon, could be considered Queen of France, and the name of her former husband may have proved embarrassing. Thus, Boileau considers that the importance of the *Roman comique* lies only in its criticism of the heroic novels. However, as a true Classicist he does not condone the burlesque, stating in his famous *Art poétique:*

> But this low style the court at last despised,
> And scorned the folly that they once had prized,
> Distinguished dull from natural and plain
> And left the provinces to Typhon's reign.[38]

Boileau then condemns Scarron and the burlesque to the same fate as another Classicist, Molière, had condemned *préciosité:* to be read only by provincials, those that have no taste.

Voltaire, in the eighteenth century, agreed with Boileau, and extended the condemnation of *Typhon* to the *Roman comique.* In the *Siècle de Louis XIV* he describes Scarron's works as follows: "His comedies are more burlesque than comic. His *Virgile travesti* can only be excused if we think of him as a buffoon. His *Roman comique* is perhaps the only one of his works which still pleases people of taste but they like it only as a gay, amusing and mediocre work, just as Boileau had predicted."[39] In the nineteenth century, the famous critic Charles Augustin Sainte-Beuve, an admirer of Madame de Maintenon, mentions her husband only in passing in the *Causeries du Lundi* (1851–62). Discussing Poussin's derogatory comments on receiving Scarron's *Typhon,* Sainte-Beuve states: "Here we find a quiet scorn, such as high and noble beings conceive for deformity which tries to think and exert itself."[40]

Poussin's reaction has already been discussed. Sainte-Beuve's statement is just a further alienation between Scarron and the admirers of the loftiness of Classicism. In the same volume, Sainte-Beuve mentions Saint-Amant, whom he classifies with Scarron. However, Sainte-Beuve then clarifies his statement: "I have listed Scarron. It would not be right to place him with Saint-Amant. The latter was of different stuff. Scarron has a bright mind, and has gaiety; but is prosaic, platitudinous, and has a banal facility which won him honors among the bourgeoisie of his time. Saint-Amant is a poet. . . ."[41]

While Boileau and Voltaire threw out Scarron's works from the court and sent them to the provinces, Sainte-Beuve sends them to the bourgeoisie. Their judgment is the same: they are not lofty enough to be read by the aristocracy. Furthermore, the charge of banality here leveled is not new. Voltaire had already stated that the *Roman comique* should be read only for amusement. Thus, so far, Scarron is regarded as a burlesque poet. His only merit is to destroy the heroic novel through his *Roman comique.* His novel lacks unity and has nothing to say. It should be read only for amusement.

Some Romantics, however, disappointed with the Neoclassical authors, attempted to find seventeenth-century works they might admire. One such author was Théophile Gautier. He was a follower of Victor Hugo and consequently paid close attention to the doctrine of the grotesque as expressed in the preface to *Cromwell.* Hugo stated that in antiquity the principle of the grotesque was an alien one so that few works presented it. Only in the nineteenth century did it flower. Following this lead, Théophile Gautier looked for early attempts in French literature. He then published a work entitled *Les Grotesques,* bitterly stating that "The majority of those poor devils with whom we have concerned ourselves in the past, would be totally unknown to us, if their names had not been mummified in some *hémistiche* of Boileau."[42]

The tenth and last portrait of *Les Grotesques* is that of Paul Scarron. Gautier first condemns the epoch: "The influence of Louis XIV was not always a healthy one in the literature and art of his time. The wig of the great king dominates excessively. Majesty, etiquette, convention, almost eradicated nature. . . . Everywhere cold regularity was a substitute for the charming disorder of life. . . . Louis XIV had a horror of truth in anything, particularly in art."[43]

Opposing these ideas is the figure of Paul Scarron with the burlesque, which is, to Gautier, the same as the grotesque discussed by Hugo. His praise of Scarron reads as follows: "Paul Scarron is, in a way, the Homer of the clownish school, the one who represents and personifies the *genre;* he was a stereotype of the movement even in his physical appearance. Byron, head of the satanic school, had a cloven foot like the devil; Scarron, head of the burlesque school, was badly formed and hunchback like a figure of Bamboche. The deviations of his verse were mirrored in the deviation of his spine and his members."[44]

Gautier's admiration for the grotesque was coupled with his admiration for Spain. He journeyed to that country and on his return published a description of his trip. Thus, he felt he had many things in common with Scarron. It is not surprising that his *Capitaine Fracasse* is an imitation of the *Roman comique.* It should be noted that Gautier's admiration for Scarron was based on the concept of the burlesque. Thus, although he is now viewed favorably and not exiled to the provinces, he is still regarded as a burlesque author only.

In the second half of the nineteenth century, two important

editions of the *Roman comique* appeared, with respective prefaces. The first was Victor Fournel's edition in 1857. He calls the *Roman comique* "le chef-d'oeuvre du burlesque cul de jatte."[45] Paul Bourget, in the preface of the 1880 edition, states, "Scarron does not know how to begin a book."[46] He also considers him a forerunner of Naturalism,[47] a term close to burlesque but definitely removed from romanesque. In these editions, then, Scarron is regarded as a burlesque poet who is not a connoisseur of the craft of fiction, thus explaining the different attitudes and types in his novel.

Critics and historians of French literature during the second half of the nineteenth century possess similar attitudes. André Le Breton, for example, includes Scarron in the literary Fronde and assures the reader that the burlesque poet "composed his book without a plan or preconceived ideas. His work has no more unity than the lives of his heroes."[48] Ferdinand Brunetière includes Scarron in an essay called "La Maladie du burlesque."[49] Finally, Paul Morillot's and Henri Chardon's works have already been discussed. They are in the mainstream of Scarron criticism.

The early twentieth century provides no changes in this type of criticism. G. Reynier has a chapter on the *Roman comique* in his work *Le Roman réaliste au XVII siècle*. He ascribes the lack of order in the narrative of the novel to the burlesque: "Even if his health had permitted him to write in a less intermittent fashion, Scarron was not a man to impose on his work a regular development, and certainly his use of the burlesque did not help to discipline his fantasy."[50] Reynier goes further and specifically blames the interpolated stories and the *récits* for some of this disunity: "The action, already lacking unity in itself, is rather often broken in the Spanish manner by short stories which have no relation to the action and which are quite different in character. The action is even interrupted by the story of Destin...."[51]

Emile Magne has an even stronger statement to make about these interpolations in his biography of Scarron. While discussing the anonymous note in which the author takes credit for the four interpolated stories, he states, naming the anonymous author: "Cabart de Villermont in his 'Anonymous Note' prides himself on having convinced Scarron to place in his *Roman comique* the short stories drawn from Spain. His influence in this respect was deplorable."[52]

A recent study, R. Cadorel's *Scarron et la nouvelle espagnole dans le Roman comique,* views the changes made by Scarron on the Spanish tales without relating them to the rest of the novel since "the action in the *nouvelles* remains entirely different from that of the *Roman comique,* and it would be foolish to look for a unity between these tales and the novel, a unity which never exists."[53]

Thus, criticism of the *Roman comique* has been along similar lines for three centuries. The novel has been called comical and burlesque. It has been included in histories of the Realistic novel. It lacks unity, thus resembling the picaresque or conforming to the burlesque. The interpolations are extraneous to the plot and are only included as concessions to the romanesque taste of the times. This concession is viewed as a mistake.

Three modern critics have departed from this repeated interpretation. The first has been G. Hainsworth in *Les "Novelas exemplares" de Cervantes en France au XVII siècle.* Although Hainsworth agrees that the *nouvelles* are included to satisfy the romanesque taste of the times. he does point to a certain unity: unity of style. Scarron, he points out, uses the same devices in the composition of the *nouvelles* as in the rest of the novel.[54]

Another critic, M. Roland Mortier, although warning that "the *Roman comique* is not a unified and rigorous work like the *Princesse de Clèves,*"[55] does find a single but complex vision of reality: "Reality in Scarron's mind is a complex and contradictory structure where the generosity of Destin and the fidelity of Dorotée are linked to the bad jokes of La Rancune, to the medicine joke antics of Ragotin, to the oedipal charms of Bouvillon, and to the assassination of Doguin."[56]

More important in this respect is the work of Ernest Simon, "The Function of the Spanish Stories in Scarron's *Roman comique.*" The author states as his purpose the attempt to link the four stories to the general structure. However, he only discusses the first one, the "Tale of the Invisible Mistress," and concludes that these tales are a parody of the heroic novels. He also mentions the *récits* and discusses Destin and Ragotin as hero and antihero, while the hero of the interpolated tale performs a different function: "Scarron has shielded Le Destin's and l'Estoile's world of high minded sentiments; but he provides through the traditional device of the interpolated love stories a purely literary presentation of love with which the comedy of Ragotin can interact."[57] He further clarifies this statement: "The purpose of all this banter, and of the link between Ragotin and the Spanish stories, is the confrontation of two extremes. Because they are nothing but fiction, contrivance, pure invention, the tales are privileged to portray a world whose inhabitants have no other business but love, and where they can pursue this exclusive business without interruption from the usual contingencies of life, which are eliminated by the author-creator's providential intervention. This situation is the exact reversal of Ragotin's predicament, where the love quest is continually frustrated by an endless series of petty contingencies. Scarron has succeeded in including in his novel both the romantic extreme of a conventional literary treatment of love, and the equally extreme burlesque of that literary convention."[58]

Ernest Simon's parallel is an interesting one. In fact, it is the first time a critic has studied any type of relationship other than stylistic between the *récits,* the *nouvelles* and the present action of the *Roman comique.* However, he has relied too heavily on the "Tale of the Invisible Mistress," disregarding the other three *nouvelles.* He mentions the tale of Destin without thoroughly discussing it or trying to bring in the other *récits.* Finally, he has not compared Scarron's text with the Spanish originals in order to see more clearly Scarron's changes and try to explain them as an effort to fit these stories into the novel. However, it does point toward new possibilities in Scarron criticism.

To conclude this sketch of the history of critics of Scarron's novel, the *Roman comique* has been regarded as a work devoid of unity. The interpolated stories and *récits* are regarded only as concessions to the romanesque, and the style and thought is considered burlesque. This creates a work for amusement, devoid of ideals. This critical attitude has been maintained until the present. However, a few modern critics have departed from this view. First of all, Hainsworth pointed to a unity of style. Then two articles appeared, attempting to find a further unifying factor. Such a search will be again undertaken in the next chapter.

CHAPTER 3

The Roman Comique *as a Unified Work*

I *A New Approach*

EMPHASIS on Scarron as a burlesque author, placement of the *Roman comique* as early as the seventeenth century in the realistic and humorous vein, and the search for Spanish sources mainly in the picaresque tradition, have fostered a disregard for some aspects in the work which are unrelated to these assumptions. The purpose of this chapter is to momentarily disregard all past assumptions such as the episodic nature of the plot, and the tradition of the comical and burlesque, in order to focus attention on the novel as a whole, taking into account the history of its composition. After such an examination is completed, the burlesque qualities of the novel will be reassessed.

A cursory glance at the outer structure of the novel immediately reveals a definite pattern if each of the two parts is compared to the other. It becomes apparent that each contains *récits* of a markedly romanesque tone. These narratives are interspersed through the present action of the novel. The present action has a very narrow setting and time limit, while the *récits* cover a lengthy period of time and the action rambles through different areas of France and Europe in general.

Such a method of composition, as will be demonstrated, resembles the techniques of the Classical theater. It would then be useful to compare the structure and techniques of the novel with the concepts of Classicism. Another question to be investigated would be the genesis of the *Roman comique* since it may shed some light on the structure and techniques of the novel. How did the author conceive this novel; did he have a particular model in mind? This second question is inevitably tied to Cabart de Villermont's statements. The importance of *Don Quijote* has already been demonstrated. The search for sources should start here, and the relationship between the two novels clarified, particularly the presence of two main characters, as Ragotin is not subordinate to Destin. Parallelisms in characters should also be brought in at this point.

Cabart de Villermont's statements are also significant in the inclusion of four interpolated stories. Did he provide Scarron the stories? It is important not only to point out the Spanish originals but to compare these to the French versions. The changes made by Scarron may provide a clue to his reasons for including them in his novel. This analysis would then permit a discussion of statements which regard these inclusions as concessions to the romanesque.

Viewing the general structure again after having examined the purpose of the *récits* and the *nouvelles,* one main factor becomes evident: there are more actual pages in the *Roman comique* dealing with romanesque adventures per se than with the present action or disgraces of Ragotin. And, even in the present action there are the usual kidnappings and recognitions of the heroic romances. Thus, the burlesque tone of the novel must be brought into question. The lack of unity and episodic plot will be finally dealt with, by showing evidence of interaction between the interpolations and the main text.

In conclusion, these investigations dealing with the possible existence of a Classical structure, a romanesque tone and a unity of action must be weighed against critics' previous assessments. A new, balanced interpretation should be achieved making allowances for both the burlesque and the romanesque, keeping in mind Scarron's evolution from one to the other in the latter part of his life.

II *The Novel as Epic: The Search for a Classical Model*

The seventeenth century looked back to the Classical authors of Greece and Rome as their teachers and models. Epic, tragedy, and comedy became the major genres. They were written according to the rules set by the ancients, as reinterpreted by the moderns. In tragedy, for example, the concept of the three unities was upheld as unquestionable, and these unities were attributed to the writings of Aristotle. Pierre Corneille states: "It is necessary to observe unity of action, place, and time; that, no one doubts."[1] Although many dramatists accepted these principles, their interpretation became a matter of great controversy, leading Corneille again to state "and perhaps to make a play succeed nowadays it is not enough to have studied the books of Aristotle and Horace."[2] Paul Scarron, a dramatist himself, considered Corneille the best

dramatic author in France. These rules and the attitude of imitation
would thus be found in his writings.

Yet, what is the relationship, if any, of these rules of the theater
to the novel? Seventeenth-century critics, in praising the dramatic
genres of comedy and tragedy, as well as the epic, and thus following
Aristotle's *Poetics,* downgraded the importance of the novel.
Novelists reacted by trying to find ancient models on which to base
their works and thus make them valid in an age of Classical imitation. The preface to one of the heroical novels, *Ibrahim* (1641),
written by Georges de Scudéry, presents the conclusions reached
by novelists about their art. It is a guideline in the art of prose fiction
during the Classical age, and offers many parallels to the rules of
the theater. Georges de Scudéry begins by accepting the Classical
preconceptions: "The works of the spirit are too significant to
be left to chance; and I had rather be accused of having failed consciously than of having succeeded without knowing what I was
about. . . . Every art has certain *rules* which by infallible means lead
to the ends proposed."[3]

The idea of art as having definite rules is accepted. The next question is: who knows these rules? The answer, again, follows Classical ideas, and echoes the dramatic treatises of the epoch: "As
we can be learned only through what others teach us, and as it
is for the last comer to follow those who go before, I have concluded
that in drawing up a plan for this work I must consult the Greeks. . .,
and to try by imitating them to arrive at the same end which these
great men proposed to themselves." The next step is somewhat
more difficult. If it is true that the ancients are the models artists
must imitate, and the ancients praised only the theater and the
epic, what is the place of the novel? Georges de Scudéry followed
many commentators of Aristotle in stating that the novel is simply
an epic in prose. In this he is supported by Philip Sidney and Julius
Caesar Scaliger. It should be recalled that Torquato Tasso stated
explicitly that love (as opposed to war) can be the main concern of
the epic. Among his examples he lists the *Aethiopica* of Heliodorus,
which is not an epic, but a romance, thus totally blurring the differences between the two genres.

The task of the novelist now becomes simpler. All he has to do
is study the epic to determine the rules that guide its composition.[4]
The first rule of composition, according to Scudéry, is unity of
action, in this paralleling the *Poetics* of Aristotle. He states: "I

observed that in the famous romances of antiquity, in imitation of the epic poem, there is one principal action to which all the others are bound, which rules the whole work, and to whose perfection all the others only contribute." This main action, in the romance or epic in prose, usually consists of a marriage. Like Tasso, Scudéry refers to Heliodorus: "And to pass from the poem to the romance, which is my chief concern, in Heliodorus, the marriage of Chariclea to Theagenes." In *Ibrahim* the main action, according to Scudéry, is the marriage of Justinian and Isabelle. Bishop Huet, in his famous treatise on the novel, would reaffirm this concept by stating that the main action of the prose epic is love. A glance at the *Roman comique* would convince the reader that Scarron was following at least this first principle. Destin, the hero of the novel, is in love with Estoile. Yet, circumstances keep preventing their marriage, which would assuredly be the denouement of the novel. As will be seen later, other love relationships serve only to reinforce and parallel the love of Destin and Estoile. Ragotin, for example, does not detract from this love. Instead, he serves to show its seriousness of purpose, idealism, and moral strength, when contrasted with his ridiculous actions and flighty and superficial attitudes. The main action, then, in *Ibrahim,* the *Aethiopica,* and the *Roman comique* is the love of the two main characters which will lead after many contingencies to marriage. Other actions, such as the reverses of Ragotin, it should be noted, are permitted by Scudéry and the Classicists as long as they contribute to the "perfection" of the main action.

Unity of action is the central concern of romance or epic. Yet, this action must be arranged artistically. Rules exist for this arrangement, and in this, the moderns should also imitate the Classical authors: "With incomparable skill they have begun their story in the middle, so as to create suspense for their reader from the very opening of the book." To begin *in medias res* means to withhold information from the reader. This creates suspense by adding an atmosphere of mystery to all that is said or done with reference to the past.

Scarron follows this idea. He begins the *Roman comique* with the arrival of a troupe of players in the town of Le Mans. The reader knows nothing of their background, particularly that of the main characters, which is essential to the progress of the intrigue. Thus, the reader is immediately puzzled by the relationship of Destin and Estoile, since he realizes that they are not brother and sister as they pretend to be and that they also appear to be of noble origin, while posing as traveling actors. Scarron uses this principle of withholding information from the reader to create suspense in many other instances. Destin and Estoile are always afraid of their "inveterate persecutor" (p. 62)[5] of whom the reader knows nothing; and Scarron also states that Destin arrived in disguise in order to evade this villain from the past. The reader is assured of the mysterious man's evil intentions when, in the adventure of the litters, it is made clear that he is attempting to kidnap Estoile. Suspense is also created at the death of Doguin, La Rappinière's valet, who has a private discussion with Destin before he expires, and the reader is told: "But Destin alone knew best of any what he ought to think of it" (p. 24).

Scudéry proceeds with his discussion of rules to be applied to the romance by stating: "and in order to keep the story within reasonable limits they have (and I following them) made it last only one year, and given all the rest in indirect narration." It is not possible to determine the time length of the *Roman comique* since Scarron never finished his novel. Yet, it is obvious that he intended to minimize the time length of the present action, and following the advice of Scudéry, place the rest of the events in indirect narration or *récits*. These narrations present the lives of the main characters up to their arrival at Le Mans. This certainly cuts down on the time length of the novel. There is one main indirect narration in each of the two parts of the novel completed by Scarron: the first part presents the lives of Destin and Estoile; the second narrates the adventures of La Caverne and her daughter Angélique. This *récit* in the second part is not as long as that of the first part and is complemented with that of Léandre, which serves to parallel the first part by presenting the lives of a pair of lovers, in this case Angélique and Léandre.

The concept of the unity of time is also present in the Classical theater, and the *récit,* usually a long discourse by a messenger or valet, has the same function as in the novel. Of the three main unities discussed by Corneille, only the unity of place is not discussed by Scudéry. In the *Discourse on the Three Unities* Corneille had stated: "I should willingly grant that everything taking place in the same city possessed unity of place."[6] Scarron, although not required to follow this rule since it is not mentioned by Scudéry, comes very close to putting into practice Corneille's principle, since most of the action does take place in the city of Le Mans. At any rate, it all takes place within the province of Mans, while actions occurring in other cities and even other countries such as the adventures of Destin in Rome, Paris, and The Hague, are included in the *récits.* The interpolated stories also take place in other lands.

Verisimilitude is another principle espoused by Scudéry and followed by Scarron. The people of Mans certainly behave in a manner typical to their province, and characters behave according to their station: it is impossible not to recognize in Destin the manners of an aristocrat, or in Ragotin those of a country lawyer.

Scudéry also states: "I do not overwhelm my hero with the prodigious number of accidents which happen to some others, for I feel they depart from verisimilitude. . . . It is better, in my opinion, to separate the adventures, to make different stories of them, to give them separate heroes." In the *Roman comique,* Scarron jokingly states: "The stroller Rancour, one of the principal heroes of our romance—for one alone will not serve our turn; and since there is nothing more perfect than the hero of a book, half a dozen heroes, or such as would be thought so, will do more credit to mine than a single one. . ." (p. 16). And indeed, his novel is peopled with many different characters who, following Scudéry's precept of verisimilitude, experience their own adventures, very much in keeping with their personalities: nothing could be further removed than the adventures of Ragotin and those of Destin, thus pointing out the great differences in their personalities and station.

It is then possible to perceive a definite method of composition when one looks at the *Roman comique* in the light of the Classical precepts. As opposed to the picaresque tradition, Scarron tries to minimize the episodic nature of the plot by commencing *in medias res* and adding *récits,* which, as will be shown later, parallel the present action of the novel, thus creating depth instead of a simple linear progression based on chronology. Each part of the novel parallels the other also: each contains two interpolated stories and indirect narratives relating the lives of a pair of lovers. Parallelism will also be seen in the characters.

The *récits* and *nouvelles* are of definite romanesque tone. It is significant that, taken together, they constitute more than half of the novel. The rest, or present action, constantly refers back to the indirect narratives. Thus, the present action, although including many comical adventures, is held together by a romanesque past, and a parallelism to be studied later, which exists between the fictional *nouvelles* and this action. As in the Classical stage, main events occur outside the theater, while characters on stage learn of these events by messengers (here the indirect narrative or the *nouvelles*) and react to them. The present action can then be seen only as a commentary on the true main action which is indirectly related. Indeed, most of the struggles of Destin and Estoile are presented in this indirect manner.

III Don Quijote *as Genesis: The Function of Destin and Ragotin*

The outer structure or manner of composition has been discussed above. The next problem is what the author is trying to present by means of this structure. One way of discerning the answer to this question is by discussing the literary origins of the *Roman comique,* in other words, its relationship to the *Quijote,* since as stated above, it is the basic literary source of this novel.

The years 1649 to 1651 mark a turning point in Scarron's life, as stated in Chapter 1. His bent for the burlesque is curbed while his interest in the romanesque becomes more pronounced. Both points of view are present in all his writings; this transitional period only serves to change the emphasis from one to the other. It should be recalled that among the events in his life which may have triggered such a change are his relationship and eventual marriage with Françoise d'Aubigné, his interest in the philosophy of Gassendi, his friendship with Cabart de Villermont, and more important, the Fronde. Faced with a movement that paralleled his attitudes in fiction, Scarron reacts by rejecting the burlesque and listening to the romanesque advice and adventures of Cabart de Villermont. Cabart dissuades the author from such a difficult task as translating the works of Gassendi. He suggests in turn that Scarron look at Spanish literature, where he has found so many models already, for something he may imitate or translate. In fact, knowing the ideas of the poet, Cabart suggests that he translate *Don Quijote.* Scarron rejects this idea since the work had already been translated. However, this contributed to the creation of the *Roman comique.* Although he already may have been thinking about a novel, this suggestion from his friend may have given his idea a new form. The quest for justice in the name of love would be appealing to this epoch in Scarron's life: the chaos and injustice of the Fronde incited Scarron to search for the impossible dream, to take Françoise to America where, by creating a new society, they could lead an idyllic life. In fact, Scarron imagined the climate of America might even cure him of his disease.

In this thought, Scarron may have been paralleling the life of Cervantes who was imprisoned: a lack of justice when he considered his heroism at Lepanto. Scarron, also incarcerated, but in a prison of useless flesh, sought to present his plight to humanity in the same manner as the Spanish author. However, instead of combining his sense of futility together with the aspirations of the human race in one character, Don Quijote, he created a dichotomy of feeling by presenting the reader two characters: Destin and Ragotin. His novel will lack the character development present in *Don Quijote* through the interaction of the knight and his squire: Destin and Ragotin are two different attitudes which cannot, in the mind of Scarron, be combined or resolved. Although they will comment by contrast they will always be apart. The romanesque and the burlesque, both present in the mind of the French author, do not seem to be able to resolve their differences, although we have a final rejection by Scarron of the sense of futility and an affirmation of the ideal which must triumph if order is to be established through justice.

Critics have recognized the existence of some similarities in both works, mainly, the similarity in some humorous chapter headings which tend to minimize the art of the novel and suggest an informal approach (which is in reality absent from both novels), and a similarity in purpose, that is, the ridicule of an existing type of fiction. While Cervantes ridiculed the novel of chivalry, Scarron mocked the heroic romance, a not-too-distant relation to the former.

But, as stated above, Scarron, owing to personal circumstances and knowledge of Spanish literature, was aware that Cervantes' novel was more than just an attack on chivalry, so that the concern for the meaning of justice and the power of love are discussed by both, mainly in the attitudes of the main characters, but also in the structure itself. This last point will be taken up later.

There are, in addition, other superficial similarities. One of these is the inclusion of interpolated stories. These, states Cabart de Villermont, he provided for Scarron. It is very possible that Cabart

de Villermont suggested the inclusion of stories in the manner of
Cervantes, and it is also possible that he provided him with some
stories. The choice of which stories to use, however, belonged to
Scarron: he did not use four stories as stated by Cabart; instead
he used five, as will be shown later. Notice also the similarity in
geographical names: Le Mans and La Mancha. It was in La Mancha
that Don Quijote acquired his illness: "se le secó el cerebro";[7]
it was in Le Mans that Scarron was stricken with a disease that made
him change his life: a man that enjoyed life so much was converted
into a mere spectator. Ragotin, in a sense, mirrors the affliction
of Scarron. He represents the sense of futility, the incomprehensible
lack of justice in the world, the disharmony that must be ordered
by the human mind. Ragotin is Scarron's reaction through the burlesque. He is the commonplace; he lacks the imagination which
transcends the sensual world, and in his struggle to accomplish
this through imitation, he fails miserably. He is the man who cannot
cope with his condition and adds to the world's the chaos of his
own self. It is the early Scarron fighting only with the burlesque.
It is important to note that structurally Ragotin exists in the present
action of the novel, the present condition of man.

  Some may think to compare Ragotin to Sancho Panza. Out-
wardly the comparison is successful, since both share an admiration
for an ideal they find difficult to comprehend. However, they are
vastly different. Sancho is able to teach as well as to learn. Ragotin
has nothing to teach since he is not part of reality either, and he
has no one to look up to except his books which he tries to imitate
mechanically to satisfy his vanity. He is an entirely negative character. The idea of Ragotin is not derived from the character of
Sancho. It represents the negative aspects of Don Quijote: the hero
of La Mancha faced with Andrés. Scarron then, comments on
Cervantes' work, by dissociation. Like many readers he admires
the ideals of the Knight of La Mancha, but he is also aware of the
futility of his quest: He rights no wrongs in his agonizing pursuit
since it is the world which carries him while he thinks he is correcting it. Ragotin knows he must love because his books state this;
however, he does not know to whom he must direct his feelings
(or the feelings he has read about). La Rancune must point out to
him the beauty of Estoile and tell him this is whom he loves before
he is aware of it. Ragotin is then carried by men and events while
he attempts to follow fiction. This is pointed out by Scarron when

he compares Ragotin to Phaëton: "We left Ragotin planted on the pummel of a saddle, not knowing how to behave himself, and much perplexed how he should get off. I scarce believe the defunct Phaëton, of unhappy memory, was ever more troubled with his father's four fiery steeds, than was at this time our little lawyer, with this one tit, on which he nevertheless sat as quiet as a lamb. That it did not cost him his life, as it did Phaëton, he was beholden to Fortune, whose caprices would be a fit subject for me to expatiate on, were I not in conscience obliged to release Ragotin from the imminent danger he is in" (p. 144).

The ever-present control of Destin is contrasted with Ragotin's fall from the horse which caused a great deal of laughter. Destin, on the other hand, is the impersonation of fiction in this world. He is very much like the heroes of novels without consciously trying to imitate them. The chaos of situations does not seem to sway him. Thus, his name: destiny. He knows what he wants and he imposes by hard work the order of his imagination into the society. Like Don Quijote, he has a lady who is the motive of his actions. Estoile, however, is an almost ideal woman, not only in the imagination of the hero, but in fact. Destin follows his star to the logical conclusion of marriage and happiness, which Scarron was not able to conclude. His adventures are markedly different from Ragotin's. The events in his life are mysterious, romanesque, and he always controls the outcome so as to always appear a hero, even if fate has not yet rewarded him. We are convinced, however, that fate will grant him happiness in the end.[8]

Although Destin may appear to the reader a fictional hero, it is significant that he moves in this world. The focal point of the *Roman comique,* like that of Don Quijote, is the inn, this being another obvious parallel between both works. The innkeeper in the Spanish novel must participate in the knight's fiction in order for the novel to advance. He must play the role of the lord of the castle and knight Don Quijote. In the *Roman comique* the innkeeper participates in Destin's fiction in a very different way: by observing Destin's theatrical performances. Nothing else is required of him. While the hero of La Mancha, himself a fictional character, must transform the fictional reality into fiction taking it another step beyond our sphere, the hero of Le Mans knows when he is performing and when he is "living." He transforms the inn, not by his imagination, but by a real action. In presenting a play he makes the audience aware of another reality beyond their own. His role, then, is to extend people's vision, not to distort it. Thus, Destin is a hero because his vision of life is more complete than that of the rest of the protagonists. Ragotin is the opposite. He is the tragedy of the burlesque: the futility of his quest stems from a lack of understanding. In seeking a love he does not understand but can only imitate, Scarron makes the reader become aware of Ragotin's presumption.

It should be pointed out that the enlargement of the vision of life, which according to Scarron is provided by the romanesque, does not mean a rejection of the sensual world: Destin lives in the inn, and not in a secluded castle. Like Don Quijote, he is also subject to its temptations. The episode of Don Quijote and Maritornes is paralleled in the French novel by Destin and Madame Bouvillon. It is ironic that the clumsiness of Ragotin provided Destin a means of escaping this temptation. Although Scarron creates an ordered vision of life, he is well aware of its inconsistencies.

Ragotin can also be seen as a social commentary. He steals aristocratic sensibility from books. Idyllic feelings are fine as long as one understands or is part of the culture that creates them. The middle class was attempting at this time to borrow aristocratic feelings in order to feel equal. This is satirized in many works of the time, as pointed out above, such as in the *Précieuses ridicules* and the *Bourgeois gentilhomme* of Molière.

Before concluding this analysis of the main protagonists of the novel, something should be said about some of the other characters. Although Scarron tells the reader over and over again that there is no order in his work, the balance and parallelism which exist in the different supporting characters of the novel are again proof that this simplicity and lack of order are only apparent, as in life, and the reader must order events in fiction, as Scarron orders them from life.

Ragotin is paralleled by Roquebrune. His faults are the same. He even partakes in the adventure of the horse: he falls just like Ragotin. Roquebrune, like Ragotin, attempts to be a man of letters, an artist, but fails miserably. He also loves, but his love must, like Ragotin's, turn to disaster, since it is only a love stemming from fictional imitation. In contrast to these two characters stand Destin and Léandre, both actors but of aristocratic origin. They are in control of their destinies. Their loved ones are both almost ideal

females: Estoile and Angélique. To balance the fictional extremes
of Ragotin and Roquebrune are La Rancune and La Rappinière,
who represent a total involvment in the sensual world coupled with
a degree of misanthropy. Destin and Léandre stand in the middle
as examples. This parallelism will be discussed further when the
interpolations are compared to the main text.

IV *Spanish Sources and French Interpolations: Changes in tone*

Paul Scarron includes four interpolated *nouvelles* based on
Spanish sources in his *Roman comique*. Cabart de Villermont claims
to have provided Scarron these four tales, which is an inaccurate
statement. In composing his four interpolated stories, Scarron
used five, and not four, Spanish sources, as will be seen later. It
is then very probable that Cabart simply provided Scarron with
many Spanish texts and that the author chose those he thought
would fit his novel. This freedom of choice is essential to our consid-
erations since it will be shown that Scarron was very careful in his
changes and in the placement of these tales. It would be impossible
to attempt to discuss all the changes made by Scarron to the original
versions in the space available here, and to analyze the reasons
for all these alterations. This I have already done elsewhere[9] and
will try only to summarize here some of the more important changes
and give a few examples.

The two stories in the first part of the *Roman comique* are taken
from a very prolific Spanish writer, Alonso de Castillo Solórzano,
who is best remembered as the author of picaresque novels. He
wrote in addition many collections of *novelas* which are far removed
from the picaresque and fall in the realm of the romanesque. They
deal mainly with courtship: its adventures and conceits. The first
interpolated tale in the *Roman comique,* "The History of the
Invisible Mistress," is derived from the third *novela* in a collection
entitled *Los alivios de Casandra* published in 1640. Castillo
Solórzano titles his story "Los efectos que hace amor." The second
nouvelle included by Scarron has two sources. The first half is
taken from "A un engaño otro mayor" also from *Los alivios,*
the second *novela*. But, for the second half of his tale Scarron goes
elsewhere for inspiration: he uses a different version of the same
story also by Castillo Solórzano. It is found in the form of an interpolated story, "A lo que obliga el honor," in a picaresque novel

published two years after *Los alivios: La Garduña de Sevilla.*
This is Castillo Solórzano's most popular work, and was translated
into several languages soon after its publication. In fact, d'Ouville,
an enemy of Scarron, translated it into French in 1660.
The second part of the *Roman comique* was published in 1657,
after Scarron had begun the publication of his *Nouvelles tragi-
comiques;* thus he had more experience in the art of translating
nouvelles. This second part also includes two interpolated stories.
The first, "Le juge de sa propre cause," is based on a *novela* of the
same title written by María de Zayas y Sotomayor, a contemporary
of Castillo Solórzano, which appeared in her collection, *Novelas
amorosas y ejemplares* of 1637. For the second tale, "Les Deux
frères rivaux," Scarron goes back to the *Alivios de Casandra* and
imitates the first tale, "La confusión de una noche."

There are some types of changes that occur uniformly in all
four stories. These can be discussed before taking each *novela*
and trying to determine the major changes that are made by the
French author and the reason for these. As in the rest of the novel,
the French author strives to impress the reader with his offhand
attitude and informal approach. Scarron states in the narrative
that he is not sure how to continue his book: "For one chapter
draws on another and I do with my book as some do with their
horses, putting the bridle on their necks and trusting to their good
conduct" (p. 60). In other words, he leads the critic to complain
of lack of unity and of impertinent disorder in the intrigue.
Cervantes, as stated previously, had done the same in *Don Quijote.*
Scarron stresses the point too strenuously to be believed. Even in
the comparison of writing to the man being led by a horse, the
reader may divine irony, since he is aware of the adventure of
Ragotin and the horse. The very nature of the action, in which Destin is in control of his destiny while Ragotin must follow wherever
fortune may lead him as expressed in the adventure of the horse,
certainly could leave the critic little doubts on the fact that Scarron
was not sincere in this statement and that perhaps he was trying to
point to his relationship to Ragotin. Even if this were not the case,
Scarron's other reason for this offhand attitude would be obvious.
He was also reacting against the ornate style of preciosity and of
the heroic novels, which he in fact ridicules in the first interpolated
story when he calls *Le Grand Cyrus* "a book that has the best fur-
niture in the world" (p. 40). When this offhand attitude is applied

to the *nouvelles,* it gives the impression that we are listening to
a tale being recounted.

That Scarron had the original before him at all times and that
he reworked it patiently never enters the reader's mind. This effect
increases the credibility of these romanesque tales and heightens
the interest. Some examples of how this is achieved should be given.
In "L'Histoire de l'amante invisible," Scarron affects to be uncertain
as to the historical background of the tale. The poet states: "He
performed wonders at the public games, which the Viceroy of
Naples entertained the people with, upon the marriage of Philip
the second, third, or fourth, for I have forgot whether. . ." (p. 32).
Castillo Solórzano states categorically that his tale occurs during
the reign of Philip IV.

This informal attitude serves at times to add to the humor or
satire in the tale. These two elements are also present in all the
stories. For example, the fourth interpolated story, "The Two
Rival Brothers," contains a statement that, in addition to increasing
the informal attitude of the novelist, satirizes the inclusion of
endless *billets* in the novels of the time: "The gallant cavalier wrote
the next day to his fair mistress, and had an answer suitable to his
wishes; but I cannot pretend to give you a sight of the letters, by
reason that none of them ever came to my hands" (p. 319). Needless
to say, Castillo Solórzano includes the *billet* and not the humorous
statement.

Scarron believed that a short humorous sentence can affect the
whole meaning of a story. "The History of the Invisible Mistress"
deals with the romanesque and ideal love of Porcia for Dom Carlos.
He goes for a long time adoring a lady he has never seen. He is
faithful even when kidnapped by a beautiful princess (who later
turns out to be his invisible mistress), and she tests his faithfulness
constantly. After many secret rendezvous in dark streets and many
unsolved enigmas of love, the novelist ends the tale with the marriage
of the hero and heroine. While Castillo Solórzano is content to
record their marriage and conclude his tale, Scarron adds, "It is
said they got up late the next day, which I am inclined to believe"
(p. 49). Such a statement destroys the solemnity of the occasion
as presented by the Spanish author and presents the couple in a
completely different light: no longer are they the untouchable
heroes, but simply people. By destroying the fantasy of the tale,
Scarron ridicules the heroic novel.

Paul Scarron also eliminates what he thinks to be needless details in the Spanish original. For example, the detailed description of Naples at the beginning of "Los efectos que hace amor" is absent from the French version. Descriptions of dress and appearance are many times lacking in the French versions also. The endless conversations between the hero and his mistress found in María de Zayas and in Castillo Solórzano are reduced in the French version, since Scarron was definitely opposed to the *précieux* salons with their endless conversations. The reader may at this point recall Sainte-Beuve's statement mentioned above, which, although it considers Scarron only as a burlesque poet, does point to his dislike of the *précieux*.[10] The reader can find a good example of this type of change in the first conversation between Dom Carlos and the invisible lady at the church.[11]

The French poet also tries to increase verisimilitude, a characteristic much discussed in the Classical age. For example, in "The Judge of Her Own Cause," when Sophie is disguised as a man, she takes with her a servant who is also a woman dressed as a man. The reader is told "he" was the only one allowed to dress Sophie. This is absent in María de Zayas. Scarron also tries to explain why Sophie made a good soldier, while Zayas never thinks twice about making this frail woman into a manly hero.

Many comparisons and allusions are also absent in the French text. They abound in the Spanish versions. The mention of Cupid, for example, that is made in "Los efectos que hace amor,"[12] is absent from Scarron's version. In "The Impostor Outwitted," when Dom Fernand and his *valet* go to sleep, Scarron simply states: "and both he and his man falling asleep . . ." (p. 152). Such a simple statement is derived from the following description: "We gave ourselves freely to Sleep who, like a thief of the senses, came called by weariness."[13] In the third tale, Scarron is content to state that Dom Carlos was the apparent author of the kidnapping. The version by María de Zayas contained a mythological allusion: "He was the author of the theft, the Jupiter of this beautiful Europa."[14]

Sententious sayings are also eliminated by Scarron. In "The Impostor Outwitted" Castillo Solórzano states: "Jealousy—like magnifying glasses—makes things appear larger than they really are."[15] This statement is absent from the French version.

It can be said, then, that in general Scarron simplifies the Spanish text, making it more clear and concise. The serious style disappears to allow for informal story telling with instances of humor and satire. A final example will serve to show the differences in the versions. It is the description of the princess in the "History of the Invisible Mistress." First, the Spanish version:

> The lady pulled off her mask and showed a heavenly miniature, or so did don Carlos think. In the beautiful space of a proportionate and white forehead, he discovered two irises, jet black and polished: arches with which love assures more conquests than the bow used to have souls surrender. These arches served as adornments to two beautiful and wide-open black eyes which glowed more than the sun. The cheeks were dressed in purple and snow, the mixture of these colors being so divine that nature admired the hands that thus created them. The beautiful cheeks were divided by a line of good proportion that increased her beauty, and in whose vicinity rested a divided carnation: such was the beauty of her lips. Guarding them were two rows of pearls more perfect than those engendered in the South. The chin did not detract from the portrait, but was a beautiful increment to her divine perfection. The Atlantis of this heavenly miniature was a gentle column of crystal, her divine throat. It was adorned with the enamel of graceful veins arranged in such a manner as to create mysterious characters with which love had written that this divine subject was the *non plus ultra* of beauty.[16]

Scarron's version:

> As the spoke these last words she pulled off her mask, and showed Dom Carlos the heavens with all their glories, or if you please, a heavenly miniature: the finest head in the world, supported by the best shape he ever admired before; in short, a person all over divine. By the freshness of her complexion one would not have thought her to have been above sixteen years of age; but by a certain free and majestic air, which young people generally want, she appeared to be near twenty. (p.43)

These stylistic changes bring the *nouvelles* interpolated in the *Roman comique* to resemble the rest of the text, so that the reader finds no abrupt transition between the adventures of Ragotin and those of Dom Carlos. The tone of the work is then even, due to Scarron's changes of the Spanish original. In addition, there are other changes which are related to the action of the stories and that are made to fit the interpolations into the main text so that the reader may perceive a certain unity of thought. These changes, together with the relationship of the interpolations to the rest of the text, and to each other, will now be discussed, taking each tale separately.

V *Interaction of Interpolations*

The first tale, "The History of the Invisible Mistress," is the story that suffers the least change when adapted into the French. At first glance, the changes appear to be purely stylistic, but its position in the novel, and the character of the narrator give us a clue as to its purpose. The narrator is Ragotin; this will be the only novel recounted by him. At first, he had a reluctant audience since they were all aware of his lack of literary talent; yet when he finished, he was greeted with "a general applause" (p. 50). The first question would then be: if Ragotin is to be ridiculed in the novel, why does he succeed in this endeavor? Because the story is told, not so much to ridicule him at this point, but to give the reader insight into his character. After all, Ragotin had just been introduced in the previous chapter, and it would have been pointless to have a digression in the midst of a description of the antihero's character.

What is the relationship between Ragotin and the story he tells? Chapter XI immediately offers the explanation. Ragotin takes Rancour to a tavern where he attempts to present the image of a poet capable of the sensibilities of the hero in a heroic romance. He wants to join the troupe of actors because he is in love with one of the actresses. The little country lawyer will give up his career to compose sonnets to his beloved. This, it should be recalled, is exactly what Léandre did: he left school and his high position in society to follow Angélique. What is the difference between the two? Léandre is a member of the aristocracy, and his feelings are genuine. Ragotin is only imitating that which he cannot understand, but he feels is superior. Proof of this can be found when Rancour asks him which actress he loves and Ragotin does not know:

"But which of them?" quoth Rancour. The little man was so disordered for having said so much, that he answered, "I don't know." "Nor I neither," said Rancour. This reply cast him into greater disorder; insomuch that with a bewildered look he said, "It is, it is—." He repeated the same words five or six times over again; at which the stroller growing impatient, cried, "I like your choice, she is a very beautiful person." This put him quite out of countenance, insomuch that he could never tell which he loved most; though it may be he knew nothing of the matter himself, or that his passion was rather lust than love. At last Rancour naming Mrs. Star, he said it was she with whom he was in love. For my part, I verily believe that had he named either Angelica or her mother Cave, he would have forgot the blow he had received with a busk from the one, and the age of the other, and given himself body and soul to the very first that Rancour had named. (p. 57)

Ragotin does not know what lady he loves. He is only in love with the idea he had read in books, as in the case of Quijote. The worship of women like Astrée who could banish Céladon with just one word, was a literary convention at the time. Ragotin was trying to imitate this fiction and thus convince himself of his own worth. The choice of the tale of Dom Carlos is then an appropriate one: the hero himself must be told how to act, while the invisible mistress controls his actions; for example, when she first sees him she tells him that he must serve her and he agrees. She is indeed an invisible goddess, an Astrée who demands service out of a man who does not even know what she looks like. In return, she gives only the mystery of love which, however, she does not possess and is to be found only in the imagination of the lover.

Thus Ragotin and Dom Carlos share analogically in the delusion of the epoch as found in the novels of the time. They must love, but this being only an ideal for them, the object is imposed on them by outside suggestion. Ragotin delights in telling the tale and then falling in love. Yet, while Dom Carlos is a fictional character, Ragotin lives in this world, according to Scarron. He attempts to re-enact a fictional tale in a world which is not bound by the precepts of his imagination. In Chapter X Ragotin is shown his own folly. One of the listeners finds a little book in the little lawyer's pocket which contains the original tale, while Ragotin has been trying to convince his audience he had written it. Thus, in this episode Scarron presents Ragotin with his own falseness. He is an imitation, a copy, and not a real human being. Just as he borrows from a book to increase his literary merit, he also borrows from fiction his convictions. He is always discovered as a fraud.

If indeed Ragotin is worthy of ridicule, why did the audience applaud a tale that stands as an objective correlative of his personality? Dom Carlos as Léandre is a member of the aristocracy. These games of love as fictionalized by Castillo Solórzano are part of the amusements of the upper classes. The bourgeoisie, as already pointed out, and as ridiculed by Furetière, attempted to copy these concepts, but were, according to these authors, unable to separate the convention and the game from the realities of existence. Thus the tale of Dom Carlos is part of the milieu and should be applauded. Ragotin's attitude, however, should be deplored. His literary ambitions are also to be deplored, and when emboldened by his success he states that he wants to change the *nouvelle* to a *pièce à règles* the reader is immediately reminded of Javotte in *Le Roman bourgeois* as she enters an aristocratic salon and describes the type of sonnet she prefers.

In addition to the placement of the story, Scarron gives other clues as to his attitude within the story itself. These will be in the manner of humorous statements and constitute a superimposed comment on the already existing interrelation between the main text and the fictional story. These statements can appear in the text of the short story even if Ragotin recounts it, because Scarron states: "You will find the said story in the following chapter, *not such as Ragotin told it,* but such as I had it from one of the hearers. Therefore you must know that it is not Ragotin now who speaks, but myself" (p. 31).

Scarron is making sure the reader does not misinterpret his statements. He will comment on literary conventions through Dom Carlos just as the latter has been created to comment on Ragotin. Three statements absent from the Spanish version, which is what we should presume Ragotin told, provide an insight into the author's attitudes. Discussing the typical hero of romances, and referring to their great imagination, Scarron states that they "build castles in Spain."[17] Dom Carlos need not use his imagination to build such castles: he has them in reality as a member of one of the best families in Spain. Thus, his reality is part of others' imagination. Dom Carlos lives in an ideal world, where the imagination can flourish next to reality, but his high position does not lead him to delude himself either: "Had he been of Don Quijote's humour, he would have found sufficient matter to please his fancy; and imagined to be no less than Esplandián or Amadís" (p. 41). The disease of the imagination is particularly harmful to the middle class, to Ragotin, since they must live life as it is. Ragotin, then, is transgressing the order of society by changing his role.

A second statement that is added by the French poet is indeed a warning to Ragotin and those like him: "Believe not your imagination at the expense of your judgment" (p. 39). At the end of the tale the warning comes true even for Dom Carlos and Porcia since, as stated before, the poet adds to the Spanish text: "It is said they

got up late the next day, which I am inclined to believe" (p. 49).
The tale of Dom Carlos then serves to point to the character of
Ragotin. His "madness" is one of the imagination, stimulated by
heroic romances. In this he parallels the Knight of La Mancha.
In this, he is criticized; yet Scarron goes another step and criticizes
all such novels for the concept of love they present. Although Dom
Carlos does not deserve the ridicule of Ragotin since the aristocracy
is permitted the luxury of the imagination, the author objects to
the unquestioned subservience of man to woman. Aided by the
salons of the *précieuses* (which Scarron despised), woman became
a symbol of refinement and culture which man must follow. In
this women lost their reality. Dom Carlos and Ragotin then stand
together as representatives of those whose love has no real object
but remains locked in their imaginations.

It should be recalled that the second tale, "The Impostor Outwitted," is based on two Spanish sources, "A un engaño, otro
mayor" and "A lo que obliga el honor," both by Castillo Solórzano.
The reason why Scarron went to so much trouble to compose this
tale is made clear in the previous chapter; there, Garouffière discusses literature with Roquebrune who, it should be remembered,
is a poet who resembles Ragotin. While Roquebrune praises the
heroic novel insisting he would receive no pleasure from reading
adventures which did not deal with great princes, Garouffière
praises the Spanish *novelas:* "The Spaniards had a peculiar talent
to compose little stories, which they called *Novelas,* which are more
useful, and more probable patterns for us to follow, than those
imaginary heroes of antiquity, who grow oftentimes tedious and
troublesome, by being over-civil, and over-virtuous. In short, that
those examples which may be imitated, are at least as beneficial
as those that exceed all probability and belief" (p. 148).

Garouffière, speaking for Scarron, and against such people as
Roquebrune and Ragotin, is making a plea for realistic tales which
can be more useful to mankind than the imaginary and the improb-
able romances which no one except those touched by madness
can imitate: this idea had been pointed out by authors like Sorel and
Segrais. Not that the French poet is going against the romanesque:
the Spanish tales are filled with night adventures, secret rendezvous,
and unknown or mysterious ladies. What he states is that these
adventures can be of use to the contemporary reader since they
deal with adventures that are probable, although sometimes unlikely,

and mainly that their heroes are not perfect, just human examples
of what is possible. A great prince that destroys an army single-
handed may fill the reader with admiration. This, however, will not
induce the reader to follow suit. A contemporary, a man involved
in amorous intrigues who tries to behave as best he can and succeeds,
can indeed be an example. Although the intrigue of the *novela* may
appear extremely romanesque to a reader today, or to a member
of the Parisian bourgeoisie, this was not the case for a seventeenth-
century nobleman, as pointed out by Adam: "Those sentimental
intrigues, the exchange of *billets,* the rendezvous by windows
with iron bars, the climbing of balconies, duels in the street, night
encounters, all these things which evoke today a distant and nonexistent society were for the men of the 1650's, Spaniards in particular,
but also Frenchmen, an aspect of the life which was led. Maybe
it is a somewhat superficial aspect, but it is certainly the most
dramatic, the most picturesque, the most appealing."[18]

Since Garouffiere praises the Spanish tale, and a Spanish lady,
Inezilla, tells a *novela* her former husband composed in Spain,
Scarron must present a tale with flawless techniques, and one that
teaches something to his peers. Thus he took great care in the composition of "The Impostor Outwitted." Recalling that a story begun
in medias res is superior to one told in chronological order, Scarron
begins the tale with the most surprising event in it: the appearance
of a stranger, Dom Fernand, devoid of any possessions, in front
of Victoria, a lady who was living a quiet life in the country. Dom
Fernand was found tied to a tree in the forest, and Victoria learns
from him that he had been robbed in the night when he lost his
way. In this Scarron follows "A un engaño, otro mayor." He uses
this model up to the middle of the story when Victoria arrives in
Madrid and becomes a servant of Elvire, the future wife of her
deceiver, Dom Fernand. The change of text can be explained by
other major changes in the French version, which necessitate the
alternate ending. Dom Fernand in Scarron is a gambler, a fact not
mentioned in "A un engaño, otro mayor." He wants to test his
fortune at all times. He is an impetuous man who tries to profit
all he can and give nothing. He is the supreme realist who has turned
cynic. When he sees Victoria, all he can think is to seduce her. The
reality of her physical beauty is what impresses him as opposed to
the mysterious circumstances and engaging spirit which had
captivated Dom Carlos in "The History of the Invisible Mistress."

Dom Fernand does not think of responsibility, and the word "impetuous" is a key one in understanding his character.

Victoria, in the tale by Castillo Solórzano, is a very weak and hysterical woman. In Scarron's version, the reader is impressed by her will power and her resourcefulness, which transform her destiny, bringing about her marriage, thus preserving her honor. Scarron effects this drastic change only by altering details. For example, when Victoria realizes Dom Fernand's deception, she becomes hysterical and blames Dom Fernand in her laments, in the Spanish version. She never thinks to blame herself and must be guided back into the practical world by Feliciano, an old servant who serves as her father. In Scarron, she appears cool-headed and blames herself as much as Dom Fernand and seeks a method of atonement. The servant who is the voice of reason and judgment in the Spanish version is absent in Scarron: Victoria has judgment, only in her burning passion ("It was nothing but . . . fire and flames" [p. 153]) had she given vent to her imagination and believed in Dom Fernand's pure and eternal love. Now, faced with reality, her judgment returned, she is able calmly to consider ways of amending or of atoning for her mistakes.

The story then deals not with honor as such, which is Castillo Solórzano's concern. It is mainly concerned with an action resulting out of the impetuousness of a cynical cavalier and a woman blinded by passion. This must be resolved, and, as the man is incapable of understanding love, it is up to the heroine. As in the first interpolated story, it is up to women to attain their wishes, since the men are at fault. The duel based on the principles of honor in "A un engaño, otro mayor" is eliminated, and Dom Diègue, a faithful suitor for Elvire is added, according to the 1642 version. He represents responsibility and, by obedience to social principles, succeeds in marrying Elvire, who was promised to Dom Fernand. The latter is forced to marry Victoria, righting the wrong he had done. They will live justly but not happily. Scarron, then, imparts to the Spanish novela a very timely concept: passion creates unthinking acts.

Between both interpolated stories lies the récit of Destin, a third interpolation. "The Impostor Outwitted" also resembles part of Destin's tale, the portion based on a play by Calderón (Ch. XV). There, two brothers, Verville and Sainct-Far, stand for obedience and impetuousness, respectively. Both marry at the end also: one out of love; the other out of necessity.

Destin's *récit* is also the mean between two extremes represented by both tales. While in the first tale Dom Carlos is ruled by the imagination and is brought down to reality by his marriage with the invisible mistress, in the third tale Dom Fernand is an extreme realist who must be shown his responsibilities. Both are locked within themselves and cannot love another person. The women must, then, become active and resolve the situation. With Destin, Estoile does not need to become superior. He can handle his destiny as explained above, and he is also capable of love. Thus, a balance is achieved among the three tales on the subject of love, with Destin emerging as the hero.

This mean between extremes is reinforced by the present action of the novel, where such a symmetry already exists. Destin and Estoile are again in the center, but she is flanked by two extremes. On the one hand, she is loved by Ragotin, representing the imagination; on the other, she is desired by La Rancune, a misanthropist. The same is true of Inezilla, whose husband represents Destin analogically. She is flanked on the one hand by Roquebrune, who has similar ideas to those of Ragotin, while on the other she is desired by Rappinière, who is as impetuous and cynical as Dom Fernand and La Rancune. Scarron takes care to point out these similarities before recounting the second interpolated story, so that one may realize its function in the structure.

The first part of the *Roman comique* can then be seen as a work dealing with attitudes toward love. Destin presents Scarron's point of view. His adventures are romanesque, yet they are plausible. He is able to love. Ragotin, on the other hand, represents many of the people of the salons whom Scarron detested. They only imitate fine feelings so as to impress others and themselves. They are not true individuals and thus cannot love. Their constant praise of the ideal is restricted to the world of their own imagination. Rappinière opposes the imagination and stands in the other extreme. His villainy is already reflected by the villainy of Dom Fernand. The latter's impetuous actions are only a fictionalized account of what will happen later in the novel. The passion of Rappinière will force him into unthinking acts.

The action of the first part of the novel is almost nonexistent. Scarron contents himself with exposition. Through humor, fictionalized accounts and *récits* the reader gains an insight into the major characters of the novel, mainly their attitudes toward love. The first story expressed Ragotin's ideas through Dom Carlos. Scarron then placed Ragotin in a position where he had to reveal himself as a fraud. Destin's tale restores order; and "The Impostor Outwitted" sets the stage for the second part of the novel, where the conflicts of love are released into action, which, since it is impetuous, will be unjust. Thus, the second half of the *Roman comique* will deal with justice as related to love.

The first interpolation in the 1657 book is not a *novela* but the *récit* of Caverne. Her story, dealing with the death of her father, and her mother's fear of the baron de Sigognac, parallel the present action: Angélique and then Estoile are kidnapped. This violence is caused by men who do not use their judgment. Sigognac, who was a "slave to his passions" (p. 195) and "more feared than loved throughout the country; as violent in all his actions as a governor of a frontier town" (p. 190), parallels Saldagne, the "unknown assailant" of Estoile, who bursts into the present action of the novel from the recollections of Destin's *récit*. The reader can pause for a moment with the return of Angélique, and Léandre's short *récit*. Yet even here justice does not prevail, and Léandre must journey to England to search the forgiveness of his father.

From the total lack of justice and the chaos of situations in La Caverne's *récit*, as well as in the present action, one moves to the first interpolated story, that of María de Zayas entitled "The Judge of Her Own Cause." The structure of the story has been totally reworked by Scarron. He begins *in medias res*, as he did in the previous Spanish tale; but here he does not have a model since Zayas' story is told chronologically. It may be that Scarron was competing with his rival d'Ouville, who the previous year had published a translation of the same *nouvelle* in his collection *Nouvelles amoureuses et exemplaires* where he criticized Scarron. It may be possible also that Scarron begins the tale at the moment of greatest chaos and disruption of order to point to the lack of justice that prevailed up to this point in the novel: Destin has just rescued Estoile from the villainous and passionate Saldagne. The interpolated story begins with the rescue of Sophie from the passionate Moor Hamete who was trying to rape her.

As Garouffière, a judge, and the nemesis of the novel, sends his men to arrest the other guilty party, Rappinière, he recounts this interpolated tale possibly to point out that justice must be retributive in this disorderly world but that it can be attained.

Through no fault of their own Dom Carlos and Sophie find themselves unjustly separated, which is the plight of Destin and Estoile when she is kidnapped. In her many adventures, Sophie learns (thus her name, which has been changed from the Spanish) that she must fight her bad fortune in order to achieve justice and partake of love. Justice is not prevalent, but it can be gained by effort. Dom Carlos, on the other hand, fights injustice with injustice: he becomes a thief and even suspects Sophie: he will not be the hero of the *novela*. Following his previous changes, Scarron has Sophie become the savior of justice and of Dom Carlos: she becomes the Viceroy and administers justice being in charge of the trial of the man she loves.

Destin goes through the *Roman comique* searching for justice in the name of his love. Estoile is unjustly taken from him, but Garouffière arrives and confers this justice. Dom Carlos is not at all like Garouffière. When his dreams are broken he goes to pieces and believes chance to be mistress of the universe. His attitude defeats him. Thus this tale, although ending happily with the marriage, does not sing of harmony but of disruption. It offers hope but not solace.

The last tale, "The Rival Brothers," is the only one where the hero and heroine are mutual in their love. Love here becomes an interaction between two people, as in the story of Destin. Since all is in its proper perspective the woman does not need to be the strong force in the *novela* as in the previous three. To achieve this mutuality, the French author must change the Spanish tale, where Dorotée falls in love with Dom Sanche and tries to meet him. In Scarron they meet by chance and fall in love simultaneously. This is also the reason why Scarron eliminates the terms "inclination" and "melancholy" which are present in the Spanish text: love is not to be considered in its Ovidian connotations. It is not an illness which disrupts but a social force atune with the rest of creation. The father of Dorotée, symbol of authority and the administrator of justice, undergoes many changes in the French version. For example, he does not try to force Dorotée into marriage and thus blends justice and love.

Man has found the harmony of distributive justice in this golden age which is glimpsed at the end of the novel. In this universal harmony there is no gap between justice and love. The Spanish text must again be changed, since here the hero must leave Dorotée because of the arrival of her father. In the French version the lovers part because the time set aside for the rendezvous is over. The proper measure of things and harmony of ideas prevail over dichotomies. Dom Sanche in Castillo Solórzano falls in love with Dorotée for her beauty. In Scarron it is her *esprit* which kindles the flame of love. Thus, as prescribed by Leo Hebraeus, love begins with reason and can develop into its finest form, that of honest love. In a sense, this love parallels the love of esteem mapped by Mlle de Scudéry in her *carte de tendre* but does not depend on its mechanics. Dorotée understands love: "Love shall never make me do anything contrary to my duty" (p. 316), she states, but adds also: "I am resolved . . . never to marry any man but who shall singly possess all those good qualities which are only to be found dispersed among diverse others" (p. 316). In these statements Dorotée understands first of all that love can not flourish in disharmony. Justice must accept it, since they are both ideals based on harmony. Second, she understands that love is based on virtue. The rational consideration of a person's qualities may lead to esteem, which is the very center of love. In other words, Dorotée understands that man must strive for what he wants within the limits of society: eros is only a destructive force. Sometimes authority in the name of society acts against the justice one seeks. This is why obedience and justice are sometimes opposite. In "The Judge of Her Own Cause" Sophie wanted the justice to be able to love a worthy man but was stopped by her father's authority. In this tale, authority understands justice. The father gives Dorotée a reasonable choice. The last lines of the story are significant: "The three marriages were solemnized in one day, and everything succeeded so well that there was no disagreement between either of the parties for a long while after, which you must confess is not a little to be wondered at" (p. 338). The order which has been achieved is a lasting one since it is based on all possible stabilizing factors: reason, authority, justice, and love. All other stories had ended simply in marriage, and the future left doubtful. Here, the certainty of harmony is hinted at.

The last story in the first part of the novel had reflected the violence which was to occur in the second part due to impetuousness based on blind passion. At the end of this second part, most of these violent actions have been resolved through justice, and Angélique and Léandre, Estoile and Destin, are back together, while punishment is being inflicted by Garouffière on the disrupters.

It is at this point that Scarron chooses to interpolate a tale based on harmony, which leads to lasting bonds through love. As with the last story of the first part, the French poet is probably expressing the theme of the next part. All that remains for the two heroic couples in the novel to be happy, is the approval of the authority. Somehow, this outcome is tied with England. At several points in the novel the reader is told that Estoile's father, as well as Léandre's father, lives in England. There had been times when a trip had been contemplated. Thus it is in England that the blend of authority and love would be achieved. This would restore the players to their proper roles. It should be remembered that Destin was raised in mysterious circumstances: Antoine Adam suggests that there might have been a substitution of children. If this is the case, Destin is the son of "a Scotch lord who was gone into Ireland to raise soldiers for the king's service" (p. 69).

It is significant that the re-establishment of authority to produce harmony, a proper place in society, and the proper environment for love to flourish is England, which at the time when Scarron was writing his novel, had been taken over by Cromwell and the Parliament. Destin's father was apparently fighting for the monarchic cause. It may be that such a historical situation was included to create an analogy with the Fronde which had just erupted in France, and was finally settled. The political implications of such a setting may be beyond reconstruction, since this third part which Scarron was writing at his death is lost. All that can be done is to point to its importance.[19]

The *Roman comique,* then, is a work unified by the ideas of love and justice. Its style is uniform, and the structure based on Neoclassical principles. Claims made by Scarron, and subsequently by many critics on the lack of order and unity, have been hopefully dispelled, since Scarron's main concern is the final harmony which he expected to present to the reader in the third part, and is already mirrored in the last interpolated story.

Jean Boorsch, making a case for the Greek romances and their imitation in the seventeenth century, states that literature exists as a means of expressing "fundamental dreams of humanity, of satisfying the human craving for the imaginary...."[20] In the seventeenth century, an epoch concerned with the chivalric or Petrarchan interpretation of love and the relationship of man to woman, Scarron forged his own dream which differed from the prevalent ideal. Instead, he truly follows the current of the Greek

romances, carrying it a step further. In these early works both hero
and heroine fight for their love ideal; she defends her purity while
he pursues and destroys obstacles. The *Roman comique* accepts the
view of mutuality in love and the active role of woman; yet it goes
further. It ignores the question of purity, and in the case of "A trompeur, trompeur et demi" commences with a breach of this ideal. The
reason is simply to place man and woman on equal standing: the
concept of purity, the lady that cannot be reached, elevated her.
Now the lovers only interact.

The French poet also discusses another prevalent concern of man:
his relationship to the eternal, which defines his importance.
Scarron's imagination again is akin to the early Greek prose fiction
authors. Destin and Estoile are guided by providence, which will
eventually lead them from toil to harmonious bliss. [21] As Scarron
guides his heroes in their quest for order, the reader senses the
author's concern with his own life. Contrary to other novelists
of his age, this French author places his characters in a realistic
environment. The exoticism of the setting in Scudéry and Calprenède
contrasts with the familiar Maine. Scarron imposes his dream
on the realistic panorama of his fiction.

It is from the last statement that the importance of the burlesque
or the comical in the *Roman comique* should be derived. Ragotin,
Roquebrune, and the endless little adventures are an essential
part of Scarron's experiment. Scarron's imagination creates not
only an ideal world but one ruled by petty contingencies where
Ragotin thinks of himself as a master; but the little lawyer is only
part of the panorama, and not a real individual. He may be considered a personification of the burlesque, of the frustrations of
an author who can not fully control his life. Ragotin is Scarron
without his *Roman comique,* a man deformed. He must die in the
end, just like the French author, while Destin is given happiness
with Estoile. Through the imagination of the author, their "immortality" is assured, and poetic justice has been achieved.

The style of the work corresponds then to the panorama of life.
It is light and witty. The conceits of the *précieux* have, for Scarron,
no bearing on man's concerns. They are to be ridiculed. In spite
of the low style and of the amusing anecdotes, the work retains
its serious qualities, and it blends, like a Spanish *comedia,* the different aspects of life into a cohesive whole.

CHAPTER 4

Continuations of the Roman Comique

I *Offray's Continuation*

FROM the day of the publication of the first part (1651), the *Roman comique* proved to be a very popular work. It was soon translated and was widely read in England also.[1] The public was then eagerly expecting a third part to the novel, and it is known that Scarron was working on it in 1659, since he sent a letter to Marigny which included the opening statement.[2]

It is also known that Scarron had taken out a privilege for this third part four and a half months before his death. The public knew the publication of the third part was imminent in 1660, and, when the author passed away, many thought his notes would be arranged so as to provide a proper conclusion for the romance. No such conclusion appeared, and the fate of Scarron's third part is unknown. The mystery is probably tied to his widow's actions.

Finally, in either 1662 or 1663,[3] there appeared in Lyons a continuation or third part of the *Roman comique*. It has been called the "Offray continuation"; he is not the author, but the publisher. Chardon, in *Scarron inconnu,* has attempted to discover the author of this *suite.*[4] According to this French critic, the work is by Jean Girault, a secretary to Gilles Ménage. He is the person to whom Scarron sold his prebend previous to his marriage to Françoise d'Aubigné, since he could not marry, being a canon. This conclusion, however, rests on very little evidence. Antoine Adam states that all that Chardon definitely proved was that the author of this *suite* was not from Lyons and that he lived in the region of Mans and Alençon sometime during the years 1650 and 1660.[5]

The author of this continuation must then remain unknown. This author, in the *avis au lecteur,* makes a curious statement regarding the fate of the original third part: "I have waited so long to present this to the public because I was told that a gentleman of merit was working with the notes of the author. If indeed he had attempted it, he would have succeeded much better than I; but after waiting for three years and seeing nothing appear, I ventured mine in spite of critics' censure."[6] From this statement, it can be gathered that Françoise d'Aubigné may have indeed given someone permission to work on her late husband's notes of the *Roman comique* and also that the Offray *suite* is probably of 1663, and not of the previous year, since the author states he waited three years. This *suite d'Offray* was not included in any of the Paris editions of the novel in the seventeenth century, but was included in the editions published in Lyons and Holland. The reason for this is also unknown.

In Paris the following year, the editor of *La Guerre comique ou la défense de l'école des femmes* states at the end of the work: "I advise you that M. de la Croix is ready to print a third part of the *Roman comique* that was begun so charmingly by M. Scarron."[7] No record exists of its publication. Indeed, to add to the confusion, critics are not sure who this de la Croix is. According to Fournel, it could be either C. S. Lacroix or Pierre de La Croix.[8] All that is known of the former is that he was an *avocat au parlement* and wrote two plays: *La Climène* and *L'Inconstance punie;* the latter is a work dealing with the Don Juan theme.[9] Nothing is known of the latter. To these two, why not add Philippe de la Croix? He was a defender of Molière in the quarrel over *L'Ecole des femmes.* After all, the editor of one of the many works dealing with this quarrel is the one who announces the *suite.*

French readers, then, had only Offray's version in the years immediately following the death of Scarron. It is this continuation which is still published together with the two parts of the *Roman comique* written by Scarron.[10] A reader will then associate many of the tendencies found in this conclusion with Scarron; thus, an analysis of it is in order.

The unknown author of the continuation published by Offray in 1663, as stated before, was well acquainted with the area around Le Mans, and carefully describes the players' route. He also had good knowledge of the plot of the novel as well as of the style of the author. Even small details from the previous two parts are recalled. For example, when Rancune makes a plea for Ragotin's inclusion in the wandering troupe, the continuator recalls a small incident which occurred to the little lawyer: "Whilst Olive and I were seeking after Madam Angelica, we overtook him riding upon an ass no bigger than himself, and repeating the adventures of

Pyramus and Thisbe, with so good an emphasis, that several rustics that were then going the same way, came up to him and gave so constant attention with their hats off, that they would not leave him till they came to the inn where we all waited" (p. 355). This, of course, refers to the fact that the peasants believed Ragotin to be preaching a sermon.

Many such references are found. Another example: when Ragotin rides his horse into the mud, jumps off and sinks "up to his armpits," Rancour proposes to draw him out by tying a cart rope around his neck and having the horses pull on it. Ragotin's inability to ride on a horse for a long time is reminiscent of the Ragotin found in Scarron, but to this, the author of the continuation adds the following: "This proposition made all the company laugh, except Ragotin, who was as scared as when Rancour wanted to cut his hat which was over his face when he was stuck in it," again a reference to Scarron's version.[11]

At every turn, the author is recalling passages written by Scarron. He even begins the third part in this manner: "In the last chapter of the second part of this romance, you have had little Ragotin all bloody. . . ." (p. 343). A similar recapitulation exists in Chapter VI: "You have seen in the twelfth chapter of the second part of this true story how Saldagne kept his bed in the Baron d'Arques' house . . ." (p. 372). Even literary tastes are preserved, since the lavish praise of Corneille present in the second part is echoed in this third part.

The style also imitates that of the first two parts in its humor and informal recounting of the tale. For example, when Rancour recites a *chanson* on stage with Ragotin, the author states: "At the end of every verse Rancour turned and winded Ragotin about as if he had been a puppet, making him to appear in so many ridiculous postures, as made the company laugh heartily. The rest of the song I have left out as superfluous to our romance" (p. 390). At the preparation of the double marriage of Léandre and Angélique, and Destin and Estoile, the author states: "Then was a notary privately sent for, and the marriage contracts drawn. I don't tell you the particulars of them, because they never came to my knowledge" (p. 441).

The identity of the characters is also more or less preserved. Destin, Estoile, Angélique, and Léandre remain as superior figures. Ragotin is certainly satirized, and a statement—"don't believe

your imagination"[12]—given as a warning to the little lawyer,
is certainly reminiscent of the warning present in Part I. However,
the author does not appear to have any sympathy for the clumsy
lawyer, and the adversities of Ragotin, instead of causing laughter,
appear at times to be due to cruel fortune and not to his own flaws.
His final death after the marriage of Estoile, although prescribed
by Scarron, does not seem fitting in this version.

Thus, the continuator of the *Roman comique* was well acquainted
with the two previous parts. He studied them so as to preserve
style, literary tastes, and continuation of almost every little incident.
Yet, although he mastered the mechanics of this fiction, he lacked
insight into the author's purpose, did not fully understand the
structure of the novel, and ignored many fundamental directives
in the plot.

In addition to the adventures of Ragotin, which, as stated before,
appear to be cruel at times,[13] the author attempts to bring to a
conclusion all the other threads of the novel. La Caverne finishes
her *récit,* again imitating the structure of the first two parts. This
story is well told, and the essential qualities of the baron are preserved: "This baron, who had always hitherto been of a morose
inflexible temper, was now all of a sudden changed from his insen-
sible brutality to the softest of passions, love, and that to so great
an excess, that he became even sick with the violence of it; nay
more, sick to death" (p. 381). This illness allows her to escape with
her daughter, who will marry the head of a troupe, and was named
Bellefleur; their offspring will be Angélique. Although this story
is well told, the author also had to deal with the principal characters
of the novel: Destin and Estoile. Here he fails. All that is accomplished is the death of Saldagne, the ancient persecutor of Estoile,
and her marriage with Destin. The reader is aware from the first
that the "villainous actions" (p. 376) of Saldagne must be punished
and that Destin must in the end marry Estoile. The actual facts
are beyond dispute. What the continuator does not seem to understand is that for this marriage to be successful, for Destin and Estoile
to live happily, all must be in order, and they must be in harmony
with authority, as pointed out in the first two parts. To do this
the French poet had included many unsolved enigmas in his work,
which a reader may have noticed. Destin is definitely the son of
a nobleman who lives in England. Estoile's father is also in that
part of Europe together with Léandre's. Thus, recognition, surprise,

and final pardon through love are related to that country. The reader must be shown all the relationships, which must be tied together in harmony. None of this is accomplished. We are not even told why Saldagne was persecuting Estoile, and the motivation of lust does not seem proportionate to the degree of his villainy. The persecution had started many years ago and is obviously related to the unknown past. Thus, the initial motives and relationships, which must have been surprising, are left to the reader to solve. All we are told is what we already knew, demonstrating a lack of imagination on the part of the author. The only recognition which we are shown is that of La Caverne with her brother. This adds little to the plot or to the conclusion of the story.

The continuator then fails to understand the direction of the main plot, based on past occurrences. He also fails to understand the purpose of Scarron, who wants to present a harmonious social grouping emerging in this imperfect world. Finally, although he is aware of a structure, his imitation of it is faulty. The continuator adds two *récits* to his third part, in imitation of the *récits* present in the original version. That of La Caverne is suitable. Yet, he also includes one by the prior of Saint Louis, which has no relation to the action of the novel. In addition, he includes two interpolated tales, "The Two Jealous Ladies" and "The Capricious Lady." These tales are much shorter than those found in Scarron. Their character is almost anecdotal, while the plot lacks the romanesque quality of the Spanish interpolations. The stories are told by Garouffière for entertainment after the double marriage. They have no connection with the action of the novel.

II *Préchac's Continuation*

It has been seen how a mediocre continuation and conclusion to the *Roman comique* was written and attached to it three years after Scarron's death. This *suite*, however, was not to be found in any Paris edition during the seventeenth century. The Parisians had to wait until 1679 to satisfy their curiosity as to the fate of the characters in Scarron's popular novel.

Nineteen years after the death of Scarron, Jean de Préchac (1647–1720) published his continuation. Although today he is not well known, Préchac was certainly very popular in the last decades of the seventeenth century. The heroic romances had given way to shorter works, mainly historical *nouvelles* of which *La Princesse de Clèves* of Mme de La Fayette is the best example. The sieur de Préchac was the most prolific author of this type of *nouvelles,* which combines a native historical setting (as opposed to the exotic settings of the heroical romances) with love intrigues, which, although fabulous and complex, had a greater degree of probability and immediacy than the heroic romances. This new type probably developed under the influence of the great popularity of the Spanish *novela,* which Scarron praises and utilizes in the *Roman comique.* The historical stories would then evolve into *romans de moeurs contemporains,* a development that foreshadows the literary trends of the eighteenth century. Préchac would also write this type of *nouvelle.*

Few of Préchac's many works stand out. Most critics mention *L'Héroïne mousquetaire* (1677), where under the historical guise of Christine, countess of Meyrac, the author discusses the fabulous adventures of a young lady who, looking for her lover in a male disguise, covers herself with glory on the battlefield. Préchac's importance does not lie, however, in a single work. It is his great productivity in the field that grants him a small place in the history of the French novel. Indeed, Antoine Adam states: "In the abundance of his production, Préchac reminds us of the author of *The Three Musketeers.*"[14]

The Préchac continuation of Scarron's novel is at times printed along with the Offray continuation, although it does not appear as often. Critics often tend to dismiss it also: Chardon refers the curious reader to Fournel, and this editor of the *Roman comique* devotes a small paragraph to the prolific author stating: "Préchac imitates quite well, and not without *esprit* Scarron's genre; but, instead of attempting to sustain and further develop his characters, he prefers to develop small incidents in the work, the pranks and vulgar farces."[15]

This statement, the only critical judgment on Préchac's continuation, is misleading. Scarron's two parts and Offray's *suite* contain many more pranks and *farces vulgaires* than this continuation. In fact, its romanesque qualities are more striking than the original's, thus erasing some of the humor, informality, and lifelike panorama of the original for a more carefully thought-out *cadre.* Fournel's other statement regarding this third part—the fact that, instead of following the main action, Préchac is content with elaborating on marginal anecdotes—is also misleading since this third part does not constitute a conclusion but only a continuation. The fact that Préchac intended this third part as a continuation and not as a conclusion should be apparent to any careful reader. Préchac leaves all the enigmas present on the reader's mind when he concludes his third part.

In fact, he heightens the suspense by creating an alliance between the old villain Saldagne, and a new character that is introduced, La Guyardière, who wants to marry Estoile and is infuriated by her "brother's" refusal. Thus, at the end of Part III, Préchac has brought the action to a crisis. Destin and Estoile can not go on much longer without revealing their past and disclosing the romanesque relationships through recognitions. All that is resolved in this third part are the loves of Ragotin and Roquebrune, thus making way for the true loves to be consummated. Both false lovers are ridiculed through intricate plots. Ragotin, as in Offray's third part, is persuaded that Ferdinando has magical powers. But here the aspects of magic are much more elaborate: an ointment that renders a person invisible, and a shirt possessed by devils are some of the major elements. This conspiracy against Ragotin recalls the second part of the novel, in particular the episode of the corpse. In the case of Roquebrune's love for Inezilla, his caresses are not bestowed on her, as he thinks, but on a monkey.

Préchac's work, like Offray's continuation, also follows Scarron in his inclusion of *récits* and interpolated stories. The *récit* included in this third part is that of Inezilla. The author recalls Scarron's statement that her first husband had written *novelas* in Spain, and creates his fable taking this into account. It at least deals with a main character in the work, and not with an unknown such as the prior. The interpolated tales are fully developed and are not just anecdotes thrown in almost as an afterthought as with the *suite d'Offray*. The first tale, "La Paysanne de Frescati," has as some of its elements disguises and recognitions. The fact that both Julia and Carlin who appear to be peasants, but have much *esprit,* turn out to be persons of quality and are married at the end, may parallel the loves of the disguised players: Destin and Estoile. The second tale, told by Ragotin, is entitled "La Fidèle Bretonne." Here again an absent father returns with a fortune and resolves the unhappy love situation of his son. This again may be pointing to the main plot. It may, however, be simply part of the writing conventions of the period.

As stated before, some of the humor and realism of Scarron is absent. The complex adventures leave little room for the simple, farcical episodes which added verisimilitude to the romanesque adventures in the first two parts. There are, however, some; and the chapter titles, as in Scarron, reflect this: "Qu'on n'aura point de plaisir à lire, si on n'a lu les volumes précédents" or "Qui pourra bien ennuyer."

The structure then, remains the same; some of the humor and informality are present although not as evident as in Scarron or Offray; the characters preserve their qualities, including the false loves of Ragotin and Roquebrune and the impulsiveness of La Rappinière; and finally the action seems to progress toward a future solution which takes into account not only Ragotin but also possibly Destin, if indeed the author was trying to bring the main action to a crisis at the end of his third part. If Préchac had written a conclusion, his work might indeed have been more popular than the 1663 conclusion.

It should be pointed out that two other conclusions to the *Roman comique* have been attempted. One was by "M. D. L." in 1771. These initials have never been deciphered. It follows only the story of Destin and Estoile, according to Fournel.[16] The latest was published in 1849 by Louis Barré, who included a very short conclusion in his edition of the *Roman comique*.

CHAPTER 5

The Tragicomical Stories

I *The Tradition of the* nouvelle *in France*

THE term *nouvelle* has had a long history in France. It was already in use during the Middle Ages. Its sense, however, was that of news and not of fictional tale; while in the nineteenth century it came to mean a fantastic tale in the manner of Hoffmann and Mérimée. Its use to designate a short story in the Italian manner, copying their term *novella*, derives probably from the first collection of short stories in France, written somewhere between 1450 and 1460. It incorporates this new meaning in its title: *Cent nouvelles nouvelles.*

These collections, which became very popular in France during the sixteenth century, had as their sources, in addition to the Italian *novella,* the native French short fiction of the Middle Ages, including the *fabliaux,* the devout tales, apologues, exempla, and fables. It is difficult at times to separate the native and the Italian sources since both often are anecdotal, general, very short, and meant for either amusement or for very specific and obvious instruction. As for the characters, they have no individuality and many times are only called "farmer" or "girl" without having a specific name. The humor has no subtlety, while the structure has no complexities, the tale always being told in chronological order.

This type of *nouvelle* was particularly popular around the middle of the sixteenth century. Noël du Fail published the *Propos rustiques* in 1548; there was a translation of the *Decameron* in 1545, together with translations of other Italians like Bandello and Straparola in the following years; and Bonaventure Despériers wrote the *Nouvelles récréations et joyeux devis* in 1558, while Marguerite de Navarre's *Heptaméron* appeared the same year.

With Marguerite de Navarre, the tales acquired something new. In the words of Frédéric Deloffre, "Marguerite understood, as Boccaccio had in his *Fiammetta* that amorous passion in a tale could have other purposes than the nourishing of the comical vein."[1]

The tragedy of love is portrayed side by side, in the *Heptaméron*, with the joyous anecdotes from Boccaccio's *Decameron*. The tragic tales are reminiscent of Bandello and will have a small flourishing, particularly at the beginning of the seventeenth century with Laffeman's *Amours tragiques* and Rosset's *Histoires tragiques*. However, the main body of the *nouvelle* in the sixteenth century will not evolve, but remain static, and, according to Jules Hasselman: "The Gallic spirit, realistic, mocking and licentious, which had parodied with Rabelais the marvelous legends, dominates the sixteenth century inspiration."[2] The *nouvelle* after its great popularity during the middle of the sixteenth century not only does not evolve, but is eclipsed, according to some critics,[3] together with the popularity of everything Italian. Hainsworth, in his thorough study of the *nouvelle* in France in the seventeenth century, states: "From 1555 on, there was, as we know, a strong reaction against the Italian influence. Toward the end of the century, the genre finds itself almost in a state of stagnation, and we can even perceive a considerable decline in the number of *nouvelles* produced in France."[4] The vacuum created by the absence of Italian influence would be filled in the seventeenth century by Spain. The Spanish *novela* will be the new model to imitate.

The Spanish *novela*, which was imitated in France, was not that of the early exponents like Juan de Timoneda where the anecdotal and general characteristics are still found. The French imitated the tales of Cervantes and his followers. Miguel de Cervantes, the famous author of the *Quijote*, published in 1613 twelve *Novelas ejemplares* which were immediately translated into French. Realizing the differences that existed between his work and those of his predecessors, Cervantes stated: "I am the first to have written *novelas* in Spanish, since the many *novelas* that are printed in this language are all translated from another language, and these are my own, neither imitated nor stolen: my genius created them while my pen gave birth to them. . . ."[5] Indeed, in creating his stories, Cervantes not only created original plots, as he states, he also created a new form which must be differentiated from the Italian. It superseded the earlier form in both countries.

Basic differences between the Spanish *novela* and the Italian short story include first of all its movement away from the anecdotal and toward the realm of the romanesque. This movement, however, does not remove it from reality, since it was the story of the Middle Ages which at times paid no attention to verisimilitude and included fantastic elements, while the Spanish tale was grounded on reality. Although it deals with kidnappings, elopements, and duels these romantic adventures were a very real part of life at the time, as pointed out by Caroline B. Bourland.[6]

This lengthening of the tale, filling the anecdote with interpolations, love letters quoted *in extenso,* poems, and *récits,* creates a leisurely medium in which the author can concern himself with his personages. Thus, the delineation of character is another difference between the Italian and the Spanish story, since the Spanish authors, not just narrating an anecdote, but making their works rather extensive, have time to present a character with individual traits.

Intricacies of structure are often used instead of just recounting the tale in chronological order. Like the epic and the romances, it often begins *in medias res,* immediately drawing the reader into the narrative. Finally, these tales are, as pointed out by Cervantes, exemplary. In other words, the many immoral and indecent incidents of the Italian *novella* where prelates and nuns are as guilty of sexual offenses as the marquis de Sade, are eliminated for problems of honor and courtship, where love is regarded as an ideal, and where the result is often marriage. Sorel, commenting on this in his *Bibliothèque Française,* states of the Spanish *novela* that "Ladies could read them without apprehension, as opposed to earlier ones which were much criticized, such as those written by Boccaccio which give very bad examples."[7]

Soon after the appearance of Cervantes' *Novelas ejemplares,* many Spanish authors began writing this type of story while French authors immediately translated or imitated them. In 1620, Rosset, one of Cervantes' translators, published the *Histoires graves et sententieuses,* a translation of ten tales of Trancoso. The following year, J. Baudouin published the *Nouvelles morales,* translating those by Diego Agreda y Vargas. Many such collections followed.

Some French authors tried to create works in this new manner instead of translating them or imitating Spanish originals. The first such attempt was made by Charles Sorel who in 1623 published his *Nouvelles Françaises.* He was not followed until 1656 when Segrais published his own *Nouvelles Françaises,* but from then on, original French *nouvelles* in the manner of the Spanish began to appear. They did not even have to appear in collections to compete

with the long heroical romances: as early as 1658 Ancelin published
L'Amant ressuscité singly. Discussing the change that took place
around 1660, Dorothy Dallas states, speaking of Segrais: "To
summarize, the French *nouvelles* served as transition between the
ten-volume romances and the smaller works of fiction which surrounded, and made possible the creation of *La Princesse de Clèves*."[8]

When in 1651 Paul Scarron included two interpolated stories
in the *Roman comique,* he was then including works that were
very popular at the time. Even the fact of interpolation was in
keeping with tradition, since Cervantes had done the same in his
Quijote. Possibly the popularity of these tales, and his great interest
in Spain, coupled with his new bent for the Spanish romanesque,
led Scarron to begin a series of adaptations of Spanish *novelas*
under the title of *Nouvelles tragi-comiques.* Four stories appeared
in the interval between publication of the first and second parts
of the *Roman comique.* A fifth story, together with two incomplete
tales, was published in 1663 in the *Dernières oeuvres de Scarron.*
These tales are almost translations from the Spanish, but their
popularity and influence in France at this time make of them important works in the historical context. They also serve to point
out Scarron's interest in the romanesque during the last two decades
of his life. A discussion of each individual story follows.

II *"The Fruitless Precaution" and the Quarrel with d'Ouville*

The first tale in Scarron's collection of tragicomical stories appeared in 1655. "La Précaution inutile" is a translation of María
de Zayas y Sotomayor's "El prevenido engañado," which appeared
in her *Novelas amorosas y ejemplares.* The method of translation
employed by Scarron in this and other *nouvelles* is the same as that
he employed in the translations of the interpolated stories included
in the *Roman comique:* he eliminates bombastic speeches; adds
humor; cuts down the number of allusions, comparisons, poems,
and love letters; and adds a certain informality to the style. These
tales, however, differ from the interpolated stories in that they
do not reflect any changes made to fit a particular theme—for
example, the changes in characterization found in "A trompeur,
trompeur et demi." These tales are written simply for entertainment.
No unity of ideas or purpose is to be found here. The graveness
of María de Zayas' prose disappears, but the romanesque tone

is preserved in the midst of an informal and at times humorous style. Two examples from this first tale will help to demonstrate the type of change made by Scarron. This type of change will also occur in the other tales.[9] María de Zayas, for example, includes poems and embellished statements to describe the love of don Fadrigue for Serafina. Scarron, on the other hand, makes the following statement about the courtship: "His poetry [don Fadrigue] expressed tender feelings, or maybe it was the rhymes of a poet he hired, since I never knew if he was able to compose in verse. He had a song composed about the illness of Amente, Philis or Cloris, and took along with his offensive and defensive weapons, a guitar which I believe to be the best in town."[10]

The beginning of the story provides another good example of the changes which Scarron made to the original Spanish version. Here are both beginnings: "The illustrious city of Granada, a miracle amidst the greatness of Andalucía, had don Fadrigue for a son. It is not fair that his true name and lineage be revealed since many of his noble relatives still reside there, suffice it to say that his nobility and richness were in an even line with his appearance; don Fadrigue being not only the most renowned person in his land, but also in many other lands where he was known for all these qualities." "A nobleman of Granada, whose true name I shall not reveal and to whom I shall give the name of Dom Pedre of Castille, of Aragón, or of Toledo, as you please—since one name is as good as another—and this is perhaps the reason that Spaniards, malcontent with their own name don't pass for a– . . . ."[11]

Although these changes in style are found, and the playful tone blends with the romanesque intrigue in Scarron, both stories follow the exact same plot. Dom Pedre (don Fadrigue in the Spanish version), left without parents and very rich at a young age, falls in love with Serafina and wants to take her for a wife. She feigns to be ill and has the marriage postponed. Dom Pedre, watching her house one night, sees her leave, follows her, and is witness to her conception of a child. Needless to say, he is appalled but has enough presence of mind and generosity to take care of the infant which has been abandoned by the mother. The dejected hero journeys to other regions to forget the incident. In Seville he falls in love with a widow but discovers she has intercourse with an old black servant. Dom Pedre then journeys to Madrid. There, his cousin, Dom Rodrigue, loves Virginie. This lady has a cousin,

Violante, with whom the hero of the tale falls in love. Virginie, meanwhile, marries a rich man from the Indies, but still wants to have relations with Dom Rodrigue. To do this, she insists that Dom Pedre has to come to the house along with Dom Rodrigue, so that the former can lie with the husband and pretend to be her, while she enjoys the pleasures of love with Dom Rodrigue. Dom Pedre reluctantly accepts, and spends a miserable night. The next morning he discovers that he had not slept with the husband at all but that it was Violante whom he spent the night with: the husband of Virginie was away on a trip. Dom Pedre keeps seeing Violante until one day he discovers her with another young man.

Desperate, he goes to Italy where he fights in the wars for fifteen years. On his return home, he stops to see a duchess. Her extremely clever deception of her husband forces him to decide to marry an ignorant woman: Laura, the daughter of Serafina, who has been raised by him at a convent in total ignorance of life. He marries her and, sure of her faithfulness, departs for court. On his return, he discovers that she has been unfaithful through the clever ruses of a young man and a celestina. Dom Pedre dies soon after, sending his wife back to a convent to which he leaves his great fortune. Both Scarron and Zayas end the story on a moral note, disregarding the *desengaño* of the hero: "The story of Dom Pedre was divulged after his death and exposed to those who thought that virtue can be perfect without good sense, that a clever lady can be virtuous of her own choosing, while a *sotte* can not, without the help of others, and without being well guided."[12]

Soon after the publication of the first tale, there appeared in France a collection of stories entitled *Nouvelles amoureuses et exemplaires,* which includes as a first tale, another translation of "El prevenido engañado." The collection appeared under the name of Antoine Le Metel, sieur d'Ouville. This author was an admirer of things Spanish. He had lived in Spain for seven years serving the count of Dognon.[13] When he returned to France, he brought with him a precious cargo, according to Chardon: "On his return from beyond the Pyrenees he brought with him a suitcase filled with Spanish works and, bit by bit, he placed in circulation the result of his readings."[14] His plays, based on Spanish sources, were followed by this collection of stories, which are, according to him, translated from María de Zayas. In the dedication, he promises to render into French more tales by María de Zayas in the near

future, as well as stories by Castillo Solórzano in addition to his
novel *La Garduña de Sevilla.*

At the time these *nouvelles* were published, d'Ouville was living
in Le Mans. His brother, Boisrobert, had received a prebend in
the same chapter of Saint-Julien where Scarron had held his benefice.
The abbé Boisrobert took possession of it in 1639 but surrendered
it the next year to his nephew Pierre Leprince. Thus, Boisrobert
and Scarron must have known each other at this time. Pierre Leprince, meanwhile, allowed his uncle d'Ouville to live with him
in Le Mans, where this author translated many of the Spanish
works he had brought with him. According to Tallement, d'Ouville
died in 1656. Thus, the publication of his *nouvelles* and his death
occurred approximately at the same time. The date of the original
publication of the *nouvelles* is debatable. According to Chardon,
they were published together in a collection in 1656. Hainsworth,
however, although admitting that the 1656 edition was the first
one to include all the tales, claims there was probably a separate
publication for each *nouvelle,* and that the first, fourth, and fifth
probably appeared in 1655, since the privileges and the *achevés
d'imprimer* are of that year.[15]

At any rate, although the sequence of the later stories may be
in doubt, and it is not certain which one came first, Scarron's or
d'Ouville's, it is certain that d'Ouville's "Précaution inutile"
appeared after Scarron's, since the former's publication created
a quarrel between both authors. This quarrel was continued at
the death of d'Ouville in 1656 by his brother Boisrobert, who had
already quarreled with Scarron over *L'Ecolier de Salamanque.*
Thus, in 1657 Boisrobert published his *Nouvelles héroïques et
amoureuses,* probably taken from his brother's papers, and which
duplicated again some of Scarron's works. This quarrel of Boisrobert and his brother d'Ouville with Scarron deserves further
study since many of the dates and events are still not clear. It is
certainly interesting to note that all three had lived in Le Mans
for a while and were connected with the chapter of Saint Julien.

D'Ouville was apparently trying to create a quarrel between
him and Scarron when he wrote his *avis au lecteur* to the *Nouvelles
amoureuses.* He states: "Don't be amazed, reader, if I commence
with a tale you have already seen translated by Scarron, and that
I title the same as he has, 'La Précaution inutile,' which certainly
appears a more natural title in French than the original Spanish

'Precaucionado engagnado' which translated as 'Le Précautionné attrapé.' Scarron, who certainly merits the reputation he has acquired, uses a comic style which is particular to him, and which always turns out well; but I have tried to bring out the true sense of the work, as well as the serious style of the lady I imitate, and this creates two different works. Furthermore, I tell you this lady's name, something that Scarron was not willing to do."[16] D'Ouville's accusation, then, boils down to the fact that Scarron did not tell his readers the name of the author he was translating, and also to the fact that his translation treats lightly a serious subject. Critics today have magnified such an accusation. Lena E. V. Sylvania, for example, states: "A comparison of the 'Précaution inutile' by Scarron with the 'Prevenido engañado' by Dona María de Zayas shows that the two are identical, and is an instance illustrative of the unscrupulous practice of some authors."[17] The charge of plagiarism is unfounded, first, because of the concept of imitation held in the seventeenth century, and second, because Scarron, on the title page of his *nouvelles,* states specifically that they were "tournées de l'espagnol en français," thus acknowledging his role as a translator.

D'Ouville's *avis,* together with the conspicuousness of his translation which appeared first in the collected stories, angered Scarron, who then stated in a preface:

I must add here a necessary response to the preface, which a book-selling printer or other person of such ilk felt disposed to place before the *nouvelle* similar to my "Précaution inutile" which has recently been printed under the name d'Ouville. This Preface is a great liar in many things that refer to me, insincere in French, and ignorant of Spanish since in these two words alone: "Precaucionado engagnado" there are two errors, one to have omitted the article, the other to have written *engañado* with a "g," a spelling unheard of in Spanish which always uses an "n" with tilde.[18]

Scarron also criticizes the author of the *avant propos* for the word *precaucionado,* correcting him since Zayas used the word *prevenido.* He then enters the name of Boisrobert in the quarrel stating he had already told him, prior to the publication of his own work, that he was intending to translate the "Prevenido engañado."

Just as this quarrel was prolonged after the death of d'Ouville, it was also prolonged until after the death of Scarron. A few months before his demise, the French poet had written invectives against

Boisrobert alluding to his private life. Soon after his death in 1661, Boisrobert had answered with a translation of *La Fouyne de Seville,* written by d'Ouville before his death, where could be found an interpolated story that Scarron had included in his *Roman comique.* The preface of the translation is by Boisrobert who states that d'Ouville "was the man in all of France who spoke the best Spanish and who best knew the graces of this language."[19] "The Fruitless Precaution" then became famous for the literary battle it stirred, which did not abate even after two of the three participants had died. But, in addition to the quarrel, the Scarron translation had a more important role to play in French literature. Mainly, it is the immediate source for Molière's *L'Ecole des femmes* (1662).

The characters of Arnolphe and Agnès are to be found in Dom Pedre and Laure. Dom Pedre, thinking he is creating a faithful wife, keeps Laure away from the world, and she is raised in ignorance of the ways of the world just as Agnès. Arnolphe, just as Dom Pedre, will listen with horror to her gallant adventure with a cavalier. Arnolphe and Dom Pedre find out too late that without judgment or good sense, virtue can not be perfect. Molière's comedy was a great success in its time; it also created a scandal. Like Scarron, the author combines comedy and burlesque with the romanesque. Indeed, the ending where an absent father returns with great riches is in keeping with the romanesque tradition. The astonishing revelation that the marriage of Horace and Agnès is what their parents had ardently desired might have borne a resemblance to the conclusion of the *Roman comique* if Scarron had finished it; there the father of Estoile and the parents of Destin probably were desiring such a marriage for their lost children. Thus, the spirits of Molière and of Scarron have many similarities. It should be noted also that this plot proved very popular in literature,[20] and later would be used by Beaumarchais in the *Barber of Seville.*

III *"The Hypocrites"*

The second of the *Nouvelles tragi-comiques* was also published in 1655. It is considered to be the best of Scarron's stories, yet the changes made are similar in nature to the other tales. These changes do not alter the tone of the work since the Spanish author was an expert in satire and invective: "Les Hypocrites" is taken from Alonso Gerónimo de Salas Barbadillo's *La ingeniosa Helena* (1612).

Salas Barbadillo's humor abounds in all his works, some of which can be considered picaresque novels.[21]

Although this work did not figure in the quarrel between Scarron, d'Ouville, and Boisrobert, it is of great historical importance in French literature during the seventeenth century. Molière, pleased with the success of *L'Ecole des femmes* which he had based on the first *nouvelle* of Scarron, used this second *nouvelle* for his next play, *Tartuffe* (1664). Needless to say, the controversy that the previous play had aroused was insignificant compared to the reaction to this play: it was not until 1669 that the play could be publicly presented without fear that the theater would be closed. The controversy was caused by the *dévots,* a group which according to Adam "had become a social type, like the monk or the hermit in the Middle Ages."[22] Although Molière was only criticizing the pretending Christian, the hypocrite who used religion for his own purposes, these *dévots* considered the work an attack on them personally.

The nature of the plot is episodic, recounting the adventures of Elena and Montufar, who can be considered *pícaros*. Molière then, did not use the plot in his composition, only an idea presented in the *nouvelle*. Montufar at one point poses as a *dévot* and is able to dupe the people. The conception of the *faux dévot* is what Molière took from Scarron's second *nouvelle*. The plot of the comedy may have been derived from real life.[23]

Scarron follows closely the plot presented by Salas Barbadillo, eliminating poems and bombastic speeches as well as needless descriptions. He adds some informality and humor. The work begins *in medias res*. Elena, knowing that a young man, Dom Sanche, who is to marry that night, is very rich but very passionate, and that his uncle knows of this, goes to the uncle and confesses that she has been robbed of her honor. She does not want to stop the marriage; all she wants is enough money to be able to enter a convent. The uncle, relieved that she does not want to stop the marriage and cause a scandal, gives her the money, telling her he will visit her the next day. Elena and her companion Montufar disappear before they can be found the next day with the money the uncle had provided them with. Later, when they are discovered by Dom Sanche, who has found out about the robbery, she is able to persuade him that she is not guilty, and he falls in love with her.

Elena attempts to abandon Montufar when she thinks he is

dying. Yet, he recovers, finds her and, after robbing her, ties her to a tree. She is found by Dom Sanche in this condition, but before he can release her he has to attend to a fight. Meanwhile, Montufar repents of his action and comes back to free Elena so that when Dom Sanche returns he is amazed not to find her, and attributes the "vision" to his lovesickness.

In Seville, Elena and Montufar pose as devout Christians. She goes to visit the sick every day, while he attends several masses and preaches to the poor about the Holy Sacrament. The people are so amazed at their devoutness that alms and favors pour into their coffers. Montufar is stopped on his way out of the church by a man who knows him and his deceptions. As the man attempts to accuse him, the furious mob attacks him. Montufar, giving a supreme example of humility, saves this man, confesses to every sin, and kneels to ask for pardon. He later takes the gentleman and buys him new clothes. Such an act of humility gains him the reputation of a saint.

One of their valets, however, is ill treated and goes to the police to expose their crimes. Knowing what may happen, they flee the city and go to Madrid where they are married and live from the money they made as *faux dévots*. The jealousy of Montufar, however, angers Elena. One day after supper Montufar thinks he has been poisoned and chases Elena to murder her. She is defended by a cavalier that is hiding in the house and who kills Montufar. The noise attracts the police, who take Elena and her suitor prisoners. They are later executed.

Scarron's ending differs from this conclusion. In the French version, Elena escapes before the police arrive, and runs into Dom Sanche. They go to the Indies together. This ending, although somewhat of a forced coincidence, adds to the romanesque quality of the tale and eliminates somewhat the episodic structure of the picaresque, since the main episodes of the tale are brought together in the end with the encounter between Elena and Dom Sanche. Again, such a conclusion creates the usual combination of realistic and romanesque elements that characterizes the writings of Scarron.

IV *The Innocent Adultery*

Scarron's third tragicomical tale appeared in 1656. It is based on María de Zayas y Sotomayor's "Al fin se paga todo" from the

same collection as "El prevenido engañado." D'Ouville includes the
same tale in his collection. However, it is not known which appeared
first, d'Ouville's or Scarron's version: both are of 1656. Whatever
may be the answer to this question, it apparently bears no relation
to the manner used by Scarron to recount the Spanish *novela*.
The realistic and romanesque elements are again combined.

The tale begins *in medias res*. Don García, who has just arrived
at court which is at that time in Valladolid, is walking down a
street of the city late at night when he sees a door open, and something thrown out of the house violently. When he approaches
the unknown object, he discovers it is a beautiful lady. Don García
takes her to his abode, where she narrates her misfortunes. The
lady's name is Hipólita (Eugénie in Scarron). She is married to
don Pedro (Dom Sanche), yet she secretly loves Gasparo (Andrade).
One day she is almost caught by her husband when she has given
Gasparo a rendezvous. She manages to escape detection with the
help of don Pedro's brother, don Luis. Later she finds out don Luis'
passion for her since he asks her to surrender her virtue to him in
payment for his services. The lady indignantly refuses. Don Luis,
who can not temper his passion for Hipólita, conceives a plan to
seduce her. One night he is able to send his brother away on a pretext
and then lies in his bed pretending to be don Pedro. Hipólita does
not realize the change and surrenders to whom she thinks is her
husband. When later her true husband returns, she realizes the
mistake, and rushes into don Luis' room, stabbing him to death.
Hipólita leaves the house and seeks refuge at the home of Gasparo,
who violently throws her out. It is at this point that don García
finds her. The denouement is simple: don Pedro dies, Gasparo
is murdered by servants, and don García marries Hipólita.

Scarron's taste for the romanesque is made clear in his treatment
of this denouement which he changes. He has Dom García kill
Gasparo, thus increasing his merit as a hero, and with his honor
avenging the honor of his future wife. Thus this conclusion has
a greater cohesiveness, by linking the honor of Hipólita with that
of her future husband. Dom García becomes a hero and saves
bienséance, which may be lacking in Zayas' work since Hipólita
has not salvaged her honor in that tale.

In addition to the romanesque ending, Scarron adds humor,
statements on Spanish customs, and the informality of style which
characterizes his prose works. The beginning of the story is typical

of his style: "The court of Spain was at Valladolid, and consequently the inconveniencies of those that were obliged to attend it, were greater (it being a place as famous for the dirtiness of it as Paris, if we may believe an eminent Spanish poet, who hath given us an account thereof) when. . . ."[24] María de Zayas' beginning is more formal, leaving out the realism, local color, and informality of style: "The court of the Catholic King Philip III being in the rich city of Valladolid, a name and attribute given by those who have enjoyed its beauty. . . ."[25]

At the height of suspense, Scarron again adds a humorous touch. Dom García has found the unknown lady and is conducting her to his home, curious as to what may have occurred. At this point Scarron adds the following digression totally absent from Zayas:

> Dom García put his cloak about her, and commanding his lacquey to hold her by the arm on one side as he did on the other, he soon brought her to his lodging, where all were in their beds, but one maid, who opened the door, cursing and bitterly railing at those who made her sit up so late: the lacquey, whether upon the directions of his master, or the pleasure of his quality taken in the doing of mischief, made her no answer than that of blowing out her candle, and while she was gone to light it again, calling him a hundred rogues and skip kennels, Dom García, conducted or indeed rather carried to his chamber (which was but one pair of stairs) the distressed lady.[26]

Other such small humorous digressions abound in the text, such as the observation that there is little fuel in Spain.[27] Yet, Scarron is not content with making additions to his text. He also eliminates what he considers unnecessary. As in the interpolated stories in the *Roman comique,* he eliminates many comparisons and allusions, as for example the allusion made by Zayas to Tarquino and Lucrezia.[28] This tale, then, differs little in treatment from the others already discussed, and the quarrel with d'Ouville seems to have had no effect on Scarron's attitude toward his Spanish sources.

V *"The Unexpected Choice"*

The last *nouvelle* that Scarron published in his collection of *Tragicomical Tales* appeared in 1657. It is entitled "Plus d'effets que de paroles" and its source is not to be found in the works of either María de Zayas or Salas Barbadillo. The story did not appear either in d'Ouville's collection. Yet, it seems very possible that the tale, which has an Italian setting as opposed to the other tales imitated by Scarron with the exception of "The History of the Invisible Mistress," is derived from a Spanish or Italian *novela*. Such a supposition stems from the fact that in that same year (1657), the abbé de Boisrobert, continuing the quarrel with Scarron after his brother's death, published a collection entitled *Nouvelles héroïques et amoureuses* which contains a version of this tale with the same title. This collection of four *nouvelles* also includes one derived from María de Zayas' "La perseguida triunfante" and entitled "L'Inceste supposé." The other two have no certain sources; but it is possible that "La Vie n'est qu'un songe" may have been taken directly from Calderón's play, and not from a short story based on the *comedia*.

At any rate, the genesis of "Plus d'effets que de paroles" is doubtful. All that can be gathered is that Scarron and Boisrobert imitated the same source, possibly Spanish. Hainsworth has pointed to a possible Spanish source, but it is a play and not a story.[29] *Palabras y plumas,* a *comedia* by Tirso de Molina of around 1615, has the same plot as Scarron's and Boisrobert's stories. Even the names of the characters and the setting are the same. The play may be based on Agreda y Vargas' *novela,* "La resistencia premiada" published in 1620 in his collection of *Novelas morales.* Yet, the *comedia* is closer to Scarron and Boisrobert than the tale. Another possible source of Tirso's play may be Lope de Vega's "El halcón de Federico" which is taken in turn from a *novella* found in Boccaccio's *Decameron.* Although these works deal with the generosity of a lover which is finally able to move the lady's heart, the incidents have no relation to Tirso's play.

To these sources which have already been pointed out by critics, could be added *Amar, servir y esperar,* a *comedia* of Lope de Vega which is based on a *novela* by Castillo Solórzano, *El socorro en el peligro.*[30] In this work, Feliciano saves Dorotea from robbers in a forest and from drowning. Yet, she marries an *indiano.* He turns out to be a tyrant, and Feliciano saves her again from being buried alive and from hoodlums hired by her husband. She finally realizes his merit. Such a series of incidents is certainly reminiscent of *Palabras y plumas.* Yet, the immediate source of "Plus d'effets que de paroles" can still be considered doubtful.

The plot of "The Unexpected Choice" is even more romanesque than the ones of previous stories. Mathilde, princess of Tarante, is a young innocent lady who has been ordered to marry Prosper. He sides with Roger and takes away Mathilde's principality. She is left ruined, but still loving Prosper. Hypolite, meanwhile, has saved her from drowning and from fire. As Mathilde disappears, ashamed of her poverty, and as Hypolite goes to find her, the King falls in love with Irène, Hypolite's sister, and discovers that Hypolite and Mathilde have been treated unjustly. In the end, Mathilde marries Hypolite, and Irène becomes queen of Naples.

The adventuresome plot, saturated with coincidences, does not prevent Scarron from using his usual humor and informality. The beginning of the tale is typical of Scarron's mode: "Though it be the first requisite in the writing of a story, to begin with the circumstance of Time, yet must I (who am a man of an humor by myself, and have always pretended to greater sincerity than any that ever employed themselves in writing novels) acknowledge myself at a loss as to this particular, and can only say that what I am going to relate, happened during the time that Naples was governed by kings."[31] Other touches are definitely by Scarron, the following statement may be an example: "To the great regret of all lovers of Heroick Spirits, this excellent person dies in the summer of his age."[32] Also by Scarron is the informal touch that the following statement adds: "Hippolito had a sister . . . and was not long before returned to Naples, upon some account or other, whereof I could never meet with any, and yet it might have been of greater concern to the carrying on of this story."[33]

Although the source of this tale remains doubtful, it may be said that Scarron's treatment remained the same as that of the other tales, where he blends a romanesque plot with humorous statements and an informal style.

VI *"The Chastisement of Avarice"*

A fifth story which did not appear in the collection, but was published posthumously, "Le Châtiment de l'avarice," should be included here since Scarron may have been preparing it for publication as part of the collection at the time of his death. Like two of the previous stories, it is taken from María de Zayas y Sotomayor. There are, however, significant differences: the tale is realistic as opposed to the romanesque plots of the previous tales with the exception of "Les Hypocrites"; it is also moralistic, presenting the "vice" of avarice and granting it its proper punishment. The previous tales had disregarded morality, as evinced in the changes Scarron made to the ending of "Les Hypocrites."

Yet, Scarron preserves his humor and informality, including at times statements on particular Spanish customs which may be of interest to French readers. One example will suffice, since the changes are similar to those of the other stories. When Marcos, the hero, arrives in Madrid, Scarron states: "It was the young Lad's good luck, though I know not by what charms procur'd, to be entertain'd a Page by some Grandee, or rather Prince, (for they have the vanity to think themselves such) a condition, not thought very honourable in Spain, that is, much at the same rate as that of Lacqueys in France or England." [34]

The plot of the tale is simple. As stated previously, Marcos arrives in Madrid ready to make a fortune. He becomes a page at first and slowly climbs the ladder to "success." He is a miser and saves all he earns. He even undresses without light to save on candles. This habit allows him in a short time to amass a considerable sum of money, and many are the ladies who would consider him for a husband. He declines all proposals until he is introduced to a lady who is widowed, and reportedly has at least twice as much money as he does. Marcos is properly impressed with her home and furnishings, and he immediately agrees to the marriage. He soon finds out he has been tricked. Doña Irène minus all the accessories of her toilet reveals the ravages of time. The creditors that come knocking at the door and remove all furnishings reveal her lack of fortune. Finally, don Marcos becomes aware that she does not even own the house they are living in. When he goes to search for new lodging, she and her supposed nephew who is really her lover steal Marcos' money and leave the city. Don Marcos, frantic at this discovery, is able to trace down one of their servants who assures him that his mistress can be tracked down with the aid of a magician she knows. The Spanish version concludes having the police discover the false magician. Don Marcos receives a letter from Doña Irene that she will not return to him until he collects another fortune. This kills don Marcos. Meanwhile, Doña Irène is robbed in turn and ends her life penniless.

Scarron's conclusion is somewhat different. Dom Marcos discovers the magician to be Gamara in disguise; Gamara was the one who told him about the widow and interested him in the mar-

riage. Justice arrives and, hearing the case, allows Dom Marcos
to go after Doña Irène and her lover. He finds them while they are
embarking on a ship for Naples. Trying to recover the money, he
and the coffer fall in the ocean. A fight starts between the "nephew"
and a servant. Doña Irène and her lover drown also. Dom Marcos
then dies in the act of trying to recover his money: thus the punishment for avarice becomes more striking.

Allusions, such as the one to the *Amadís* which was used as the
book of magic in the Spanish version, are absent in Scarron. Many
of the details present in the Spanish tale are also absent, particularly
in reference to the art of magic. However, Scarron follows the plot
faithfully up to the last part where he changes the ending, something
reminiscent of "Les Hypocrites." But instead of allowing the crim-
inals to go free as he had done in the previous work, he inflicts on
them a worse punishment.

It should be pointed out that María de Zayas' tale bears a striking
resemblance to a *novela* by Cervantes, "El casamiento engañoso,"
which may have served as a source. Scarron's portrayal of the miser
also resembles Harpagon in Molière's *L'Avare* (1668), but here
the relationship between Molière and Scarron is very doubtful, so
that Molière's debt to Scarron is probably limited to his use of
"Les Hypocrites" and "La Précaution inutile."

It should also be pointed out that fragments of two other tales
are found in the last *Oeuvres de Scarron:* "Histoire de Dom Juan
Urbina" and "Histoire de Mantigny." These fragments reveal the
same type of style and plot present in the five stories discussed above.

CHAPTER 6

The Theater

I *The Spanish* Comedia *in France*[1]

A S is well known and has already been pointed out, the vogue of Spanish letters in France from the early part of the seventeenth century on led to countless imitations and translations. In the field of the theater, such imitation did not gain momentum until 1640, and it was restricted to the comedy. Before that date, one can encounter isolated instances of imitation: the novels of Cervantes had been adapted for the French stage by playwrights such as Alexandre Hardy; Jean Rotrou had drawn three tragicomedies and two comedies from Lope; and Corneille had used Guillén de Castro's *Mocedades del Cid* for his famous *Le Cid* of 1636.

Although isolated instances of Spanish tragedies and tragicomedies appeared in the 1640's, the main bulk of the Spanish influence, and the greatest success encountered by French playwrights were centered around the comedy. According to Lancaster, d'Ouville "was the first dramatist to establish in comedy what may really be called a Spanish vogue."[2] The reader may remember the controversy between Scarron and d'Ouville dealing with the *Nouvelles tragi-comiques:* thus this author was not limited to imitating *comedias* but was also concerned with prose fiction.[3] At any rate, his *Esprit folet* of 1639 was the forerunner of this type of imitation. It is based on Calderón's *comedia de capa y espada, La dama duende.* D'Ouville follows it up with *Les Faussez véritez* (1642), again imitating a play by Calderón, *Casa con dos puertas mala es de guardar.* In it he even makes an allusion to his earlier play.[4] This work, like his earlier one, was a great success.

D'Ouville wrote a total of five comedies derived from Spanish sources. His last such play appeared in 1646. He did not just imitate Calderón but borrowed plots from several Golden Age dramatists such as Lope de Vega and Montalván.

The great success of Antoine Le Metel, sieur d'Ouville, gave

Paul Scarron, already interested in everything that was Spanish, the idea of writing plays based on Spanish models, and as early as 1643 he followed d'Ouville's lead. Other important French dramatists followed suit. Thomas Corneille, brother of the author of *Le Cid,* published seven comedies from 1649 to 1656 derived from Spanish sources. He adapted plays by such authors as Calderón, Rojas Zorrilla, and Moreto. Finally, Boisrobert, brother of d'Ouville, made a comeback to the theater through his imitations from the Spanish. From 1650 to 1656 he published eleven plays, out of which only two are not adaptations of Spanish *comedias.* His first such play, *La Jalouse d'elle mesme,* although based on Tirso's *comedia* of the same name, bears a close resemblance to d'Ouville's *Esprit folet* and to the first interpolated story in Scarron's *Roman comique.* In fact, Scarron may have thought that Boisrobert was also imitating Castillo Solórzano and thus included a passage in his work ridiculing Ragotin for turning his tale into a play.[5] Possibly to dispel this notion, Boisrobert later wrote another play, *La Belle invisible* (1656), which is indeed based on the short tale.

This era then, from 1640 to 1656, can be characterized in the theater as one of imitation of the Spanish in the field of the comedy. Playwrights would borrow from their neighbor across the Pyrenees and compete among themselves, creating adaptations of the same plots. The similarities already present in the cloak-and-sword plays are thus further brought together by this type of competition.

II *Scarron's Theater*

In criticism, the theater of Scarron has received a similar treatment to his other works. The comedies of the French poet are analyzed mainly for comical and burlesque elements, while the more serious intent and the romanesque tone are often disregarded. Robert Berens, for example, in his enlightening and thorough study of literary satire, states about one of Scarron's plays: "Scarron's satirical comedy has romanesque elements which his public expected. Scarron *conceded* to this taste and filled his plays with a series of romanesque adventures."[6] This type of statement is prevalent in an otherwise perceptive study: speaking of a romantic couple, Berens states that "Scarron wanted to give the public what it liked";[7] and later, discussing the *Ecolier de Salamanque,* he repeats that "Scarron made a concession to the romanesque theater."[8] Other

critics such as MacCurdy consider the burlesque "the most notice-
able feature of the Frenchman's plays";[9] but Lancaster finds that
both burlesque and romanesque derived from Spanish sources
are conspicuous in his plays.[10]

An analysis of the French poet's plays and statements on his
plays will show that he slowly evolved from a comical attitude triggered by his desire for success to a more romanesque and thought-
ful tone. However, it should be pointed out that all of his plays
contain romanesque elements, since all (except *Le Prince corsaire*)
are based on Spanish *comedias*.

The initial problem in dealing with this evolution is a statement
by Lancaster discussing *Dom Japhet:* "In his earlier comedies he
had made a romantic plot his chief concern, while adding comic
scenes in which the moving spirit was a grotesque valet. Here the
grotesque figure is no longer a valet, but the principal character,
one who seeks the hand of the heroine and whose amusing misfortunes occupy the greater portion of the comedy."[11] For Lancaster, then, Scarron moves from a limited comical interest in
Jodelet ou le maître valet (1645)[12] to a broadening of the comical
elements in *Dom Japhet* by making the hero a burlesque figure.
This is not entirely correct. Berens, in his thorough study of satire,
points out the true intent of *Jodelet ou le maître valet*. This was
Scarron's first play and was reputedly written in three weeks, as
opposed to the lengthy periods of writing involved in creating his
more serious works such as the *Roman comique*.

This play, written one year before his notorious *Typhon,* has
probably the same purpose in mind: to be successful by amusing
the public, a quality Scarron knew he possessed. As in the *Virgile
travesti,* Scarron takes a serious form of literature and weaves
laughter into it. One of the many literary conventions that are
satirized in this play, according to Berens, is the *récit*. The play
opens with a *récit* pronounced by the servant Jodelet, where he
describes at length his master's trip and its purpose. He adds how
tired he is and other trivialities, often repeating himself. His master
tires of such a lengthy *récit* and tells him to be quiet. According
to Berens, other literary conventions are also satirized in the play;
the soliloquy is travestied, and the use of *stances* by such playwrights
as Corneille to invoke material objects is ridiculed. Jodelet, in
disguising himself as the hero of the play, further travesties the
whole situation and creates an almost burlesque comedy reminis-

cent, as stated before, of other creations by Scarron of this epoch such as the *Virgile* and the *Typhon*. Lancaster, then, was mistaken in his notion that the comical in this play was restricted since it is the most satirical of all of the poet's comedies.

Scarron's next play, *Jodelet soufflé* (1647), was an attempt by the playwright to exploit the success of his now famous valet. However, it was a failure, which, according to More, was due to the "complicated and impertinent intrigue."[13] Thus, in adding romanesque qualities to his play, Scarron met with defeat. His defeat, however, was probably not in the romanesque elements per se but in his lack of ability at this point to combine more than one plot into a cohesive whole: for this play, he used two Spanish *comedias* instead of one—Tirso's *No hay peor sordo* and Rojas Zorrilla's *La traición busca el castigo*.

Even though the play was a failure, the character of Jodelet, already present in his first play, became a stock character for many such comedies and was thus immortalized. Scarron created this part for Julien Bedeau, an actor that was at this time performing in the Marais. Molière, who as we have seen owed some of his ideas to Scarron's *nouvelles,* also used this character taken from the burlesque poet: in *Les Précieuses ridicules,* Julien Bedeau played the role of Vicomte Jodelet, thus bringing to a successful peak his career as a foolish valet, cowardly, but greedy, who serves to satirize many of the aristocratic conventions of the time. As for the plot, it bears close resemblance to another of Scarron's plays, *L'Héritier ridicule.*[14]

The same year that he published the *Jodelet soufflé*, Scarron published *Les Boutades du Capitan Matamore et ses comédies.* It includes a *scène comique* and a one-act play in *vers burlesques* where each line ends in -ment. This play is significant in the history of the French theater in that it was the first one-act play to be presented on the French stage. It enjoyed a considerable success. The same year, the French poet presented *Dom Japhet d'Arménie,* which, however, was not published until 1653. According to Lancaster, "of all French plays written before 1650, with the exception of Corneille's masterpieces, *Dom Japhet d'Arménie* was the most successful if we may judge by the number of recorded performances.."[15] While his earlier plays, as has been pointed out, were a satire of the different dramatic conventions, *Dom Japhet* narrows the matter of ridicule (and does not enlarge it as Lancaster had stated) by focusing it on a

single character, Dom Japhet, the exact opposite of the heroic
figures of Mlle de Scudéry's romances; a fool who pretends to be a
gentleman, taking himself all too seriously thus enhancing his own
ridicule. He is balanced by a truly heroic couple, Dom Alphonse and
Léonore. The plot has many romanesque characteristics. This play,
then, is reminiscent of the *Roman comique* where Ragotin, a comical
figure, is paralleled by Destin and Estoile. Ridicule here is no longer
travesty or burlesque since the author is poking fun at that which
needs to be ridiculed, while the actual heroes involved in a romanesque intrigue are victorious in the end. This play can stand as the
prototype of Scarron's writings in this field. Midway between the
ideal and the travesty, it represents Scarron at his best; the public,
recognizing this, acclaimed it, and the work became as popular as his
novel. A detailed study of this play will follow in the next section
since it is so representative of Scarron.

L'Héritier ridicule, his next play presented in 1648 and published two years later, exhibits the same characteristics as *Dom
Japhet,* and also enjoyed a great deal of popularity. It marks the
end of the first period of his comedies where the comical element
plays an important role. This work was first performed in 1648.
When his next play is performed in 1654, six years later, Scarron's
approach to the theater was radically changed. Instead of a comedy,
he produced a tragicomedy, *L'Ecolier de Salamanque,* again using
Rojas Zorrilla as his source. The work lacks the usual comical
elements present in his previous ones. In the preface, Scarron states
that the story is one of the most beautiful to have come out of Spain.
He thus wants to present it in its ideal form, not debased by any
burlesque or comical elements. The only humor present in the play
comes through the valet, Crispin, an imitation of the *gracioso*
Crispinillo from the Spanish *comedia.* Thus, he does not add, but
only preserves what humor existed in the original. It is the character
of the clever valet, who could even speak some Latin phrases, and
not the seriousness of his play which exerted an influence on the
literature of the time. As for the play itself, it failed. It may be
that the public expected to be entertained by Scarron and, when
confronted with a serious play, was not interested. It may also be the
result of the quarrel with Boisrobert who wrote a play on the same
source and presented it at the Bourgogne, soon followed by Thomas
Corneille. Three plays on the same subject are not bound to be
successful. At any rate, Scarron, after trying to present to the French

public what he thought the romanesque should be like, and failing, turned back to his middle mode. But even though it failed, it seems to have had a particular importance for the author. A separate analysis of this play will be made.

From the truly burlesque Jodelet, Scarron moved to plays like *Dom Japhet,* where satire of ridiculous attitudes is paralleled by heroic figures. He finally evolved into purely romanesque writings which fail. His reaction was to return to the middle stage. His next two plays, *Le Guardien de soy-même* (1655) and *Le Marquis ridicule* (1656), are very similar to *Dom Japhet* and *L'Héritier ridicule.* However, as Berens points out, the comedy "is on a higher, more witty level."[16] At the same time he published his *Nouvelles tragicomiques,* and now that his interest in alchemy and the utopia of America were aroused, Scarron was having to write comedies in which he made concessions to the comic taste of the times.

Two plays published posthumously in 1662 show that Scarron had not totally dispaired of writing purely romanesque plays for the stage. *La Fausse apparence* and *Le Prince corsaire* are plays as serious as *L'Ecolier de Salamanque.* There are also fragments of plays he never completed. The longest belongs to a play to be entitled *Le Faux Alexandre* in which the interest of Scarron for the *Quijote,* something already discussed in the *Roman comique,* is evinced. The posthumous plays and this fragment will be discussed separately in order to perceive the new direction of his theater at the time of his death.

In conclusion, it can be stated that the romanesque interest of Scarron has always been present in his plays, since all of them except for the last one are based on Spanish *comedias* with complex intrigues. This interest was at first concealed in the burlesque style of the author as in *Jodelet ou le maître valet,* where all the techniques and idealizations are ridiculed. Presumably, Scarron was exploiting his talent for the comical at this point. The second step leads us to plays satirizing a character who is in himself ridiculous, but tries to appear as a hero through imitation of others. Most popular in this category is Dom Japhet. Scarron then turned to the purely romanesque after six years of inactivity. This change in emphasis corresponds to a similar one in his prose and poetry. It also reflects new concerns in his own life like his marriage, his dream of America, and his alchemical pursuits, guided by the adventuresome and almost romanesque personage, Cabart de Villermont. Yet, his failure here led him back to the middle stage, where his greatness lies. Here, by creating parallels between the ridiculous and the truly ideal, he is able to combine both elements, the romanesque and the comical in just such proportions as to create a pleasing and balanced effect appealing to the Classical mind. His last years were once again devoted to the purely ideal in such plays as *La Fausse apparence* and *Le Prince corsaire*. The fragment of *Le Faux Alexandre*, though, shows his interest still on the middle stage and the concern he had always shown for the figure of Don Quijote. Indeed, appearance and reality—a problem developed in the *Roman comique*—seem to be also a main element in his plays. As in the novel, characters like Ragotin imitate social and literary conventions in order to appear as romanesque heroes. They fool themselves but never the truly ideal heroes who live a romanesque life as opposed to the lowly trials and tribulations of the comical character. Dom Japhet reminds us of Ragotin, while Dom Alfonse is similar to Destin. What was said then of the quixotic characteristics of the *Roman comique* applies also to Scarron's theater.

III *Dom Japhet d'Arménie*

For the plot of his most successful comedy, Scarron turned to Alonso de Castillo Solórzano, whom he was also using at this time as a source for some of his interpolations in the *Roman comique*. According to Lancaster, Scarron's adaptation of *El marqués de Cigarral* is very free, since he "altered and added so much that two thirds of his lines are quite independent of his model."[17] Although individual lines may differ from the Spanish original, Scarron made only minor changes in adapting the Spanish *comedia*. He follows the work by Castillo Solórzano almost scene by scene and conversation by conversation, extending it into five acts. The first act contains very few changes. Scarron deletes some unnecessary speeches which lack humor, to add to the conciseness of the work. He adds a few humorous statements and changes others to fit the character of a French audience. The line of action is the same. Dom Alfonse is in Orgaz dressed as a student, trying to win the love of a peasant girl, Léonore. He is actually the son of the ambassador to Rome, Pedre de Toledo. To further disguise himself he enters the service of a fool who pretends to be a great nobleman, Dom Japhet d'Arménie, or don Cosme as he is called in the Spanish version. This character emerges as the main humorous attraction of the play, and thus the valets need not exercise their role as *graciosos*. An example of added humor occurs when the *bailli* is talking with Dom Japhet:

DOM JAPHET: What's your name?
BAILLI: I am called Alonzo, Gil, Blas, Pedro, Ramon.
DOM JAPHET: So many first names?
BAILLI: Just that many.
DOM JAPHET: My dear friend, one might suspect that you had more than one father. (Vol. 6, p.402)[18]

The next scene in the first act is somewhat changed in Scarron's version. It is the conversation held between Léonore and her "sister" Marine. Léonore avows her love for Dom Alfonse but states that she knows his true quality. A letter that fell from his pocket revealed to her he was of high quality, but that he was promised to be married to a lady in Seville. When Dom Alfonse appears, she rejects his suit although she tells him that time might change her feelings. This attitude is the rational one from a lady that has found out a gentleman's situation: if he remains and does not marry as he is supposed to, she will accept his love. In Castillo Solórzano, the motives are different, reflecting attitudes particular to Spain. There, Léonore is not aware of her nobility but is attracted to don Alfonse, thinking he is what he says, a student. She rejects him but tells him that time may change her attitude. Thus she is acting out of virtue and decorum, qualities absent in the peasant. This virtue reveals her true rank to the spectator of the seventeenth century. In choosing don Alfonse she is aware of their kinship; she realizes she has a mentality different from the *villano* in general but akin to don Alfonse's. Later, it will be revealed that this bond between them is *hidalguia*. Scarron, of course, ignores this attitude, which is purely Spanish, but, in doing so, he weakens his plot in one detail. In the third act, when Léonore is with her equals, she is able to act as a lady of noble birth without being taught. Given the Spanish idea that such actions are innate in the nobleman, there is no problem with credibility, but in Scarron's case the transition is somewhat incredible.

Scarron uses the last two scenes of the first act of *El marqués de Cigarral* to create the second act of his comedy. Here Dom Japhet comes in with his valet. When they see Léonore, Dom Japhet falls in love with her. In Castillo Solórzano, Dom Japhet had appeared when Dom Alfonse was talking to Léonore and was thus able to ask his "secretary": "Who is this peasant girl to whom you were talking?"[19] In Scarron, the exclamation of the *bailli*, "There she is talking to your secretary!" (Vol. 6, p. 416) is somewhat forced since Dom Alfonse had come onto the stage talking with Dom Japhet. Dom Japhet falls in love with Léonore, but she is able to see his foolishness, something which the *bailli* was unable to comprehend. A letter arrives at this time stating that Léonore is of noble parents but had been left in the village with all secrecy to be raised by the peasant. She must now go to take her rightful place in society. At this point, Scarron adds an extra scene at the end of the act, where, capitalizing on Léonore's knowledge of Dom Alfonse's love for her even when she was thought to be of humble origin, he creates some gallant verses. Pretending to be speaking for his master Dom Japhet, Dom Alfonse inquires if he may visit her. Her reply reveals she understands his request:

> *Dites-lui cependant qu'il aime et qu'il espère*
> *Qu'il peut se montrer tel qu'il plairoit à mon père!*
> *Et s'il daigna m'aimer pauvre comme j'étois,*
> *Qu'un pareil sentiment peut lui donner mon choix,*
> *Pourvu qu'il soit constant et qu'il soit véritable.*

(Tell him in the meantime to love and to endure/that he may appear in such a way as to please my father./Tell him if he deigned to love me when I was poor/that such a feeling may bend my decision/provided he remain truthful and constant.) (Vol. 6, pp. 423–424)

Act II in Castillo Solórzano is used by Scarron as his third act. The act is taken up with the arrival of Dom Japhet to see the prior, by whom he is mockingly given the title of marquis. The comparisons made by Scarron, absent in the Spanish version, reflect an important trait of this play. Dom Japhet is called a second "Dom Quichot" (Vol. 6, p. 428) before he arrives, while in his presence people compare him to Amadís (Vol. 6, p. 431). Thus we may notice the similarity that exists between Don Quijote, Dom Japhet, and Ragotin. As stated previously, the *Roman comique* had been a reformulation of ideas presented in the *Quijote*. In the character of Ragotin we had found some elements of the Knight of La Mancha. In Dom Japhet the same elements are present, and it can be clearly seen that Scarron had the Spanish character in mind, since he refers to him in the comedy. Dom Japhet thinks he is an Amadís. In this he resembles Don Quijote. The people laugh at his foolishness while playing along with him and calling him Amadís to his face—but Don Quijote behind his back. The antihero, if we may call him this, in the novel and drama of Scarron is based on a particular vision of Quijote. He attempts to act following a literary or ideal model which he does not resemble in the least. By taking himself seriously as a personification of this ideal which he is so far from, he creates humor.

The fourth act is the culmination of Dom Japhet's foolishness. Like Ragotin, he can not understand why Léonore (Estoile) can conceivably reject his suit. In pursuing this ideal lady, this Dulcinea, the fool meets disaster. The scene on the balcony, where Dom Japhet is stripped of all his clothes and then soaked by a full chamberpot the maid throws down on purpose from a window is the height of ridicule. In the fifth act, the actions of Dom Japhet are mainly told in *récit,* thus relegating him to a secondary role and allowing the hero and heroine of the work to emerge and play out the last facet of their love dance. In the end, Elvire does marry Alfonse, while the extra pair introduced by Scarron also marry each other with parental blessing. Dom Japhet is meanwhile sent off in a mock procession to meet an Indian princess who will marry him. Scarron's wording is at this point highly amusing:

> *L'héritier du soleil, le grand Mango-Capac,*
> *Souverain du pays d'où nous vient le tabac,*
> *Prit Coia Mama sa soeur en mariage,*
> *Du pays du Pérou la fille la plus sage,*
> *Du valeureux Mango, de la Belle Coia,*
> *Est sortie en nos jours l'infante Ahihua. . .*

(The heir of the sun, the great Mango-Capaco,/ruler of the land whence comes tobacco,/took in marriage his sister Coia Mama,/the brightest girl in the country of Peru./From valorous Mango, from beautiful Coia,/has come in our time the princess Ahihua. . .) (Vol. 6, p. 473)

The mock marriage of Dom Japhet is then paralleled by the serious marriages of Léonore–Dom Alfonse and Elvire–Dom Alvare. This last act brings back into its proper perspective the action of the play. While the foolishness of Dom Japhet is relegated to the valet, the romanesque and ideal love relationships are placed in the foreground of the action. As in the *Roman comique,* the figure of Dom Japhet (Ragotin) is contrasted to the figure of a true hero, Dom Alfonse (Destin). The latter will win his lady while the former serves only to heighten the hero's image.

Thus, it would be a mistake to call this play or the *Roman comique* a burlesque work, since burlesque serves to debase that which should be esteemed. Scarron's purpose is completely different. He ridicules that which deserves ridicule, that which is false; at the same time, he devotes attention to the ideal and romanesque. Although in this play a great deal of the interest lies in the foolishness of Dom Japhet who is another Don Quijote, Scarron is careful to parallel this mock-hero with a serious hero who is able to shape reality. Dom Japhet is throughout fooled not only by his own madness but also by other people. He appears as a puppet of the whims of society: Charles V makes him a favorite and then forgets him. Dom Alfonse, on the other hand, is able to do what he wants since he knows himself. This contrast between Quixotic madness and the true heroic ideal is essential in the works of Scarron.

IV   L'Ecolier de Salamanque

L'Ecolier de Salamanque, Scarron's first romanesque attempt in the theater, appeared six years after *L'Héritier ridicule*, the turbulent period of the Fronde lying between both publications. As stated previously, the chaos of this period may have shifted Scarron's tendencies, and the romanesque now emerges triumphant: the little humor there is in the play is relegated to the valet, Crispin, the *gracioso* of the Spanish version.

The facts of the presentation of this play are not absolutely clear. It has been claimed, and indeed it is very probable, that the simultaneous adaptation made by Boisrobert of Rojas Zorrilla's *Obligados y ofendidos y gorrón de Salamanca* precipitated a quarrel between both authors: the brothers Parfaict accuse Boisrobert of stealing Scarron's plot; but the statements of Tallement des Réaux, who lived in this period, do not confirm this anecdote. He asserts that the simultaneity of the adaptations by Scarron and Boisrobert was coincidental but that the problem was created by a lady friend of Boisrobert who interceded with the Prince d'Hancourt to have Boisrobert's version presented at the Hôtel de Bourgogne even though the comedians wanted to perform Scarron's play. Thomas Corneille's version was a later one.

If indeed Scarron knew of Boisrobert's treachery and such treachery existed, it would have seemed that he would have denounced it as he denounced d'Ouville in the preface to the *Nouvelles tragi-comiques*. But instead of complaining, the French poet mildly states that the Spanish *comedia* "was sighted by two reputable writers at the same time that I became interested in it. This did not prevent my treating it" (Vol. 6, p. 80). Scarron's only complaint in the preface is addressed to a *conjuration de précieuses:* "Beautiful ladies who are capable of directing human destiny wanted to play havoc with my fragile play . . . and compared it with unparalleled grace to mustard mixed with cream" (Vol. 6, p. 80).

Thus, Scarron first of all does not even claim to have discovered the Spanish *comedia*; second, he does not blame Boisrobert; third, he complains only against the *précieuses*. Such an attitude from a person always ready for polemics raises doubts about the fact that these two plays originated the quarrel between the two writers. What can not be contested is the existence of the quarrel in later years.

To justify having attempted to adapt the same Spanish material as two other French playwrights, Scarron makes what may be considered a very significant statement: *"L'Ecolier de Salamanque* is one of the most beautiful Spanish plots to appear on the French stage since the beautiful comedy of the *Cid"* (Vol. 6, p. 79). Scarron then did not attempt to add humor or farcical situations to this comedy in order to gain applause. Instead, impressed by its serious tone and romanesque adventures, he produced his first tragicomedy. Objecting to tragedy where he thought he could find the same type of material as in the heroic novels of Scudéry, Scarron produced for the theater what he had produced in fiction, an alternative based on Spanish forms. Although he was not successful and would return to his previous manner, this play is significant because it presents to the reader what Scarron himself enjoyed. And he never quite abandoned the idea, as will be seen in his posthumous plays.

The main question to be answered in this chapter is why Scarron chose this play, out of the whole dramatic repertoire of Spain, to show the public his taste for the purely romanesque. A clue to the solution may be found in the fact that the French poet was particularly fond of adapting *comedias* by Rojas Zorrilla. Three of his eleven plays are known to have used *comedias* of this Spanish author as models. Calderón de la Barca and Castillo Solórzano also commanded the attention of the French author, but he borrowed from them only twice. Thus, it is Rojas to whom Scarron most often turned.

Raymond R. MacCurdy, in his study of the theater of Rojas

Zorrilla, finds two very important characteristics in his plays. First, the heroine of these *comedias* is active. She is not the passive female of most of Spanish *comedia,* serving only as the *object* of love or of an honor situation. Second, Rojas Zorrilla "calls into question the validity of the basic concepts of conjugal honor as they were customarily presented on the Spanish stage."[20] In these characteristics might be found the answer. It should be recalled that Scarron complains of the negative reaction this play received from the *précieuses,* admirers of the heroic novel. These ladies—passive but all-powerful in their pinnacle of adoration—are the exact opposite of Estoile, a heroine who must toil together with Destin to achieve happiness. While *précieuses* and heroines of novels discuss the nuances of love without acting, the heroines of Scarron must cope with real life and its contingencies if they are to merit their lovers: Victoria in "A trompeur, trompeur et demi," for example. Thus, the first characteristic of Rojas Zorrilla's plays certainly blends with Scarron's ideas. This necessity for interaction also explains his changes in act five.

The second characteristic, the deviation from the prevalent concept of honor, may also have some significance. While in some honor dramas Rojas alters the appropriate conclusion to save the doomed heroine, in *L'Ecolier de Salamanque* it is the two heroes that spare each other. The key word of the drama becomes generosity bred through the admiration for each other's deeds. Following the Fronde, a period where many fought bravely and without reason, a play like this one may certainly have a great deal of significance. For Rojas, the two heroes, men of great valor and integrity are caught in a situation in which they should fight each other. But for the Spanish author, the honor code is mistaken motivation. The same is true for the French poet if we view the play in a historical context. The noblemen of France fought for something confused and meaningless. Their valor could have been wasted if they did not have other emotions such as generosity. A chaotic world of passion and incomprehensible laws can be ordered through generosity.

The plot remains the same in both plays, and Scarron follows the Spanish model very closely until the fifth act. Félix discovers that his daughter has soiled his honor. She has had an affair with a count who refuses to marry her. The father, too old to avenge himself, calls on his son. Dom Pedre meanwhile has been seeing Cassandre, the sister of the count. Her other brother, Louis, having discovered the situation, sets up an ambush. In the dark, the count discovers a lone man fighting a group of assailants and grants him sanctuary in his house. He later finds out that the man he has lodged in his house has just murdered his brother. Dom Pedre wants to wait to duel with him until he settles a matter of honor in his family, which the count does not know is his concern also. The count states he has to go on a dangerous mission. Dom Pedre insists on accompanying him to repay the count for allowing him to remain in the house. It turns out that the count's mission is to Léonore's house. They are discovered by Félix and Dom Pedre must decide whether to side with his father and avenge the honor of the family or side with the count who has saved his life. In the end, he allows the count and Léonore to escape. In the confusion, Dom Pedre is arrested. In jail he discovers a plot to kill his "enemy." Released from jail, he defends him and saves his life. Having taken care of their obligations, they must now take care of their honor and duel in order to cleanse it.

At this point the two plots change. The Spanish *comedia* has a simple denouement. Realizing they admire and owe to each other more than they have lost, the generous enemies attempt to settle their differences: the count will marry Léonore, while Dom Pedre, to atone for the death of the count's brother, will serve him as a brother by marrying his sister Cassandre, whom he loves. Although the same decision is reached in the French version, it occurs not in the thinking of the two men but with the aid of Cassandre and Léonore, who arrive on the scene. This change serves to satisfy Scarron's desire for complete interaction. Although Léonore had shown initiative in the first act, Scarron demands that love be formed only in complete interplay. Since Léonore had lost her love in the first act, it is she who must regain it.

L'Ecolier de Salamanque was certainly for Scarron a beautiful story. For him it was the ordering of reality through generosity and the flourishing of love through the interplay of hero and heroine. All the romanesque and adventuresome qualities of the Spanish are preserved in this excellent adaptation. Yet Scarron, wanting a triumph like *Dom Japhet,* would turn back in *Le Guardien* and *Le Marquis ridicule* to the middle stage.

V *Posthumous Plays*

Death came and allowed Scarron to sleep for the first time in many years before he had published or had performed two plays which he had written. Fragments of other plays also remained. This material was published posthumously, thus allowing us to judge his interests in the last years of his life. From his biography it is clear that he strayed more and more into the ideal and romanesque guided by Cabart de Villermont. From his prose we gather his strong interest in the Spanish romanesque and a curbing of all comical and burlesque tendencies. The Classical bent which will be noticed should not come as a surprise if we remember that his *Roman comique* abided by Classical standards in the structure. The influence of his wife may have been significant in these new ventures.

La Fausse apparence, one of the two posthumous plays which we have in their entirety, resembles his previous dramas in that he used a Spanish *comedia* as a model: Calderón's *No siempre lo peor es cierto.* This *comedia* is no different from others he had previously adapted since it contains the usual disguises, night encounters, overheard conversations, and other such conventions of cloak-and-sword plays. Yet what is significant is that the unities are preserved. There is unity of time, since he limits the action to twenty-four hours; there is unity of place, since the setting is an inn in Valencia; and unity of action is also preserved, since Scarron deals with only one conflict while minimizing the usual subplot. The work ends happily with the marriage of both heroic couples. The main concern of the play is the dilemma of Carlos, who loves Léonore but is convinced of her unfaithfulness. The seriousness of the dialogue and the acceptance of the rules represent major changes in the direction of Scarron's dramas.

The other posthumous play which is preserved is totally different from any other drama that Scarron wrote: there is apparently no Spanish source for it, and the plot itself does not seem to be derived from a *comedia.* Scarron calls it a tragicomedy, thus reminding us of *L'Ecolier de Salamanque;* but in fact, it resembles many of the heroic dramas of the Classical age. The unities are preserved in this work also. It is possible, as stated before, that Scarron was prompted by his wife in this matter, as she believed in the new movement. The heroic and romanesque plot, however, is different from his other works in that it deals not so much with the Spanish type of romanesque but with a closer imitation of the ancient Greek form expressed in their romances.

The plot of *Le Prince corsaire* is complex and shows many elements of the byzantine novel, including the recognition scene. Heroes and heroines behave admirably in love and war. For all the sacrifices, attempted murders, and threatened wars, the end is happy, and the two heroic couples are married to the choice of their hearts: the pirate turns out to be the prince who was thus disguised.

The seriousness and Classical care of the posthumous plays of Scarron show that he had not completely abandoned the efforts initiated in *L'Ecolier de Salamanque* and that he would have attempted again to return to this approach, since it agrees with his inclination, even though the public may have preferred his comical mode.

Of the fragments preserved, only one group is complete enough to make an analysis possible. The play was to be called *Le Faux Alexandre* and was to exploit all the devices that had made Scarron popular with the theater public. The play ridicules that which is worthy of ridicule, while it also contains the heroical couple which we assume will marry in the end despite the objections of fools and parents. Léandre loves Aminte, the daughter of Comte de la Tour, who has promised her in marriage to Felton, cousin to Aminte, a depraved individual. Léandre dresses his valet Jodelet as a gentleman, thus reminding the reader of *Jodelet ou le maître valet*, but goes further by having this "gentleman" appear to be a fool: he has read the romance *Cassandre* and thinks of himself as Alexandre. Léandre, the hero, is his "valet." This strange madness which again reminds the reader of a previous work by Scarron, this time *Dom Japhet d'Arménie,* interests the count who allows the disguised Jodelet and his master to visit him. They are thus able to talk with Aminte who, aware of the trick, favors Léandre. Meanwhile, to postpone the marriage, Léandre creates another fantasy to feed the delusions of the countess, who wants to marry her daughter only to a prince. Léandre hires a man to pose as a Transylvanian prince who is traveling incognito and who loves Aminte. Again this is the usual and very popular device utilized by Scarron: to exploit people's madness and thus gain one's ends. Unfortunately, Scarron never finished this play which would probably have been as popular as some of his previous ones. Some lines that describe the false Alexandre may be revealing of Scarron's ideas in many of his *comedias:*

Vous dites donc, Monsieur, qu'en lisant la Cassandre
Il s'est imaginé qu'il estoit Alexandre?
Du fameux dom Quichot c'est marcher sur les pas.
Dom Quichot était fin, celui-ci ne l'est pas ;
C'est un fou véritable, et qui me fait bien rire.

(You say then, sir, that in reading Cassandre/he imagined that he was Alexandre?/He is following the steps of Dom Quichotte./But Dom Quichotte was clever and he is not;/he is a veritable fool and makes me laugh.) (Vol. 7, p. 375)

As stated in the chapter dealing with the *Roman comique,* Scarron saw in Don Quijote both the fool and the idealist. Ragotin possessed only the madness, while Destin exemplified the idealism. *Le Faux Alexandre* will then be only that part of the Knight of La Mancha ascribed to Ragotin. It is from this foolishness that Scarron creates his most famous heroes, including Dom Japhet, while the heroic couple in the play serves to balance the comic and round out the figure of Quijote.

Even at this stage of his literary development, Scarron clung to the formula which had proven successful before—the blend of the comical and the romanesque. Although the poet was pursuing a road which led away from the comical in later life, toward concepts more and more removed from everyday affairs like alchemy, he still preserved enough wit, imagination, and closeness to life to be able to create in *Le Faux Alexandre*, in the Transylvanian prince, and in the countess who believed this deceit, characters that are akin to Ragotin and the foolish aspect of Quijote. His theater, then, although evolving to the romanesque, is always free to return to the middle stage, where the author is at his best.

CHAPTER 7

The Poetry

I *Scarron's Poetry*

TO his contemporaries, Scarron was known mainly as a burlesque author. Indeed, he was the most important figure in the burlesque movement. It is in his poetry that this tendency is reflected best, and yet it is also his poetry that is most carelessly written. In most cases, his poems were written to commemorate a specific occasion or to praise a particular person. They are circumstantial in nature, meant only for the amusement of his contemporaries and for his remuneration. Although Scarron's production is large, one must thumb through many pages if one expects to find something other than mere comical effect. Yet, a study of this great mass of poetry would be useful to determine the nature of his burlesque. The very circumstantial nature of his poetry, then, makes it difficult to develop as did his other literary forms. Contrary to the prose and drama, it is not as easy here to discover a progression from the burlesque to the romanesque.

In the vast material composed of *épîtres, satires,* odes, *stances, chansons, étrennes,* sonnets, *rondeaux,* and *épigrammes,* three poems stand out and are remembered in literary history. They are the *Typhon,* the *Virgile travesti,* and the ode of *Léandre et Héro.* The first was what created his first success. The second made of Scarron the leader of the burlesque. The third poem, however, has been singled out only recently by R. Berens. It was written long after the other two, in the period when Scarron had already turned to the romanesque, and in it the reader can indeed find such qualities. Thus, even though a progression cannot be found in the poetry from the burlesque to the romanesque due to the very nature of such poetry, in other words, the fact that it was written to please the public—and the public demanded wit from Scarron—it can be said that some later poems such as *Léandre et Héro* have a more tempered tone and that the comical here is blended with the romanesque. Indeed, such poems seem to have Spanish sources.

It should be noted that the burlesque tendency of Scarron is derived from Italy while his romanesque tendencies, as shown previously, are linked to the Spanish mode. As will be seen in the discussion of the *Virgile travesti,* the burlesque already existed in Italy. The Italian voyage may have provided the poet with tools for future use. Although he recognized the romanesque spirit of the city and talked with such masters as Poussin, Scarron probably also read his Italian contemporaries and was encouraged by companions on the trip to compose burlesque verses such as those found in the *chansons à boire.* Scarron, then, although somewhat influenced by the burlesque spirit he discovered in some Italians, and in this encouraged by the French public, turned finally to more romanesque concerns, basing his works on sources from beyond the Pyrenees. Although this can not be seen as clearly in his poetry, the poem *Léandre et Héro* can serve as an example for this concern.

II Le Typhon

All of Paris became aware of the genius of the crippled poet in 1644 with the publication of the truly burlesque poem, *Typhon.* This attack on mythology was also an attack on Paul Scarron's father: the counselor's partiality for Ronsard, a poet who revered the Olympian gods, should be remembered. Indeed, the poem attacks one of Scarron's favorite works, Noël Conti's *Traité de mythologie,* which had been recently translated in 1641. Chapters XXI and XXII of this book, dealing with Typhon and the giants, were the source of Scarron's poem.[1]

When Jupiter had defeated the Titans and banished them to Tartarus, he was confronted with an even more terrifying enemy, the giants led by Typhon. These were horrible creatures created out of the earth by Juno. They had one hundred heads with one hundred mouths, which breathed fire and emitted terrible cries which frightened gods and men alike. Typhon's marriage produced a host of horrid creatures, including the sphinx and the hydra. Jupiter finally incarcerated them under the earth. Their efforts to escape produced earthquakes and the famous volcano, Etna, through which they breath their fire.

From this cosmic and epic struggle, Scarron created a truly burlesque and comical poem. The terrifying creatures are seen in the beginning of the poem playing a game of ninepins on earth, the only difference between their game and that of children being that they used huge rocks, as high as the bell tower of Strasbourg. Mimas happens to hit Typhon inadvertently with one of these rocks, and the giant, in a rage, throws all the rocks he had fashioned up into the air. Unfortunately, he throws them too hard, and these rocks pierce heaven and practically destroy the abode of the Olympian gods. Thus, a cosmic war becomes a petty rivalry between giants who amuse themselves as children and gods who act as bourgeois. The description of Olympus at the time of the attack is certainly masterful beginning with Jupiter and his wife:

> *Jupiter le lance Tonerre*
> *Dormoit ayant bu trop d'un verre*
> *Et Junon qui n'avoit moins bû*
> *Dormoit sur un lit à cul nu.*

(Jupiter the hurler of thunder/was sleeping having drunk to blunder,/ and Juno who had drunk no less/was sleeping without her dress.) (Bk. I, p. 9)[2]

> *Pour Mars il prenait du Pétun*
> *Méprisant tout autre parfum:*
> *Car depuis que dans la Hollande,*
> *Où sa renommée estoit grande,*
> *A petuner il s'estoit mis . . .*

(As for Mars, he used to take snuff/of other perfumes not the slightest buff:/ For since in Holland/where his renown was grand/he had begun to snuff the stuff.) (Bk. I, p. 8)

These visions of heaven not only show the petty occupations of the gods and thus lower our admiration for them but also show anachronism, such as Mars's visit to Flanders. The placing of ancient myths in a contemporary situation also serves to debase the high tone created partially by distance. Just as amusing is Jupiter's reaction: "Et furieux comme Tyran/Jure deux fois par l'Alcoran." (And furious as a tyrant/he swears twice on the Koran) (Bk. I, p. 10). The reader is then informed that the anger of Jupiter stems not from the fact that someone had dared to molest the bliss of the heavenly abode; the motivation for his anger is more mundane:

> *. . . un furieux coup*
> *De quelque machine de guerre,*
> *A tout brisé vostre buffet . . .*
> *Tous brisez sont les verres nôtres*

> *Si qu'il en faut acheter d'autres*
> *Ou bien boire aux creux de nos mains.*

(. . . a furious blow/from some weapon,/completely destroyed your buffet . . . /All our glasses are broken,/and we shall have to buy others/or else drink from our cupped hands.) (Bk. I, pp. 10–11)

Informed of the destruction of his meal and drink, Jupiter sends Mercury to warn the giants of his wrath. Needless to say, Typhon does not fear the gods and only insults his messenger. Next day both councils, that of the gods, and that of the giants, assemble. The giants decide to attack heaven:

> *Car Typhon avoit résolu*
> *S'il devenoit maistre absolu,*
> *Aux uns de leur raser les nuques,*
> *Des autres faire des Eunuques*
> *Et distribuer aux géants*
> *Les déesses et leurs enfants.*

(For Typhon was resolute/ if master absolute,/to cut off the heads of brothers,/to make Eunuchs of others/and to distribute to giants/goddesses and their infants.) (Bk. II, p. 2)

The gods discover the giants' plan by reading the *Gazette* and the *Extraordinaire* (another instance of anachronism); their council is less resolute than the giants' and behaves like an earthly one: Neptune gets confused in his own speech; Mars pretends to be very brave and states that he alone can defeat Typhon; and soon Jupiter finally closes the session after nothing had been decided and only irrelevant speeches had been made. The following is an example of the irrelevant speeches, this one pronounced by Bacchus; the anachronisms should also be noticed:

> *Quittons, quittons la l'ambrosie*
> *Comme une viande mal choisie*
> *Et nous adonnons aux jambons*
> *Qui sont si savoureux et bons,*
> *Laissons le Nectar aux malades*
> *Aussi bien que les limmonades,*
> *Et que l'on fasse entrer céans*
> *Vin de Bourgogne et d'Orléans.*

(Let us abandon ambrosia, abandon it/as a dish little fit/and let us take up ham/so healthy and good,/Let us leave nectar to the ill/as well as lemonade,/ and let them now begin/to bring wine of Burgundy and Orléans.) (Bk. II, p. 14).

Jupiter then calls the clouds which render heaven invisible from earth. But this idea was not a very bright one—"Ce fut bien moins le dommage/des géants, que leur avantage" (It was less the defeat/ Of giants, than their advantage) (Bk. III, p. 18)—since in this darkness the giants place mountain upon mountain and thus ascend to Olympus. Wanting to see the confusion he had created, Jupiter goes to the window, but to his chagrin, he sees the horrible face of a giant. Frightened, the immortal god yells: "Miséricorde, je suis mort!" (Mercy, I die!) (Bk. III, p. 19). Luckily, the window is not large enough to allow the giant to enter. His shouts and those of his wife awaken Olympus, but the giants have already invaded the heavenly abode. Not even the thunderbolt of Jupiter can stop them.

At such a crucial point, it would be a disregard of the epic tradition not to have a message from Fortune, from an oracle which would provide a clue as to the result of the cosmic battle. And indeed, a letter arrives from earth stating that the famous Tiresias and also Nostradamus (again presenting an anachronism) declared:

> *Que les géants ses enemis*
> *Ne seroient jamais à mort mis*
> *Sans le secours et la vaillance*
> *D'Homme de mortelle naissance.*

(That the giants his enemies/would never be killed/without the aid and valiance/of a man of mortal birth) (Bk. III, p. 28)

While a messenger went to search for Hercules, a possible candidate, the giants attacked anew. The gods, seeing themselves lost, changed their forms into animals, and thus escaped the giants: it should be remembered that these giants had no great intellect and thus they could not recognize the metamorphosis (the giants had also drunk too much *vin d'Orléans*). The picture of these metamorphosed gods is truly comical: Jupiter as ram, Juno as cow, Momus as swan, Vulcan as calf, Pan as rat, Mars as hare, Mercury as stork, and so on. They flee from their abode and regroup on the shores of the Nile River. Having obtained some local clothes and changed back to their original form, the celestial beings enter the city of Memphis where they lodge at an inn in which the inn-keeper is a *cocu* and the wife a *coquette*.

The inhabitants of Memphis are not deceived by the gods and immediately recognize them. After all, they can see that instead of raising their feet to walk, the strangers seem to glide in the air. Another sign by which the inhabitants of Memphis recognized the quality of the visitors was that "leur aisselle n'exhaloit/qu'odeur qui le nez consoloit" (Their armpits only exhaled/an odour which consoled the nose) (Bk. IV, p. 6). Soon the priests were informed, and gifts were brought, among which were hippopotami.

Soon, with the aid of Hercules, the gods counterattack. Jupiter, carrying thunderbolts made in Memphis, attacks from one side and thus distracts the giants; the other gods, led by Hercules, invade the giant camp. The valor of Hercules, born of a mortal, wins victory for the gods; many giants are killed, while Typhon is held prisoner under Mount Etna. The people in the countryside of Sicily believed from that time on that the fires that come out of the volcano are but the *soupirs ardents* of the captured giant.

Scarron finished the fifth book of *Typhon* with a moral lesson which, since it was derived from the comical text of the poem, means little to the reader:

> *Ainsi presque toûjours le vice*
> *A la fin trouve son supplice,*
> *Et jamais la rebellion*
> *N'évite sa punition.*

(Thus nearly always vice/in the end finds its price/and never will rebellion/ avoid its retribution.) (Bk. V, p. 13)

This first major venture into the burlesque by Scarron is then characterized by the use of trivial detail in the presentation of a high subject. Gods appear as bourgeois, while giants are ignorant and childish creatures. The metamorphosis of the gods further debases their quality by being en masse, and caused by fear. Thus, although following the mythological tradition, Scarron changes it in detail to create a comical effect. He further debases the subject matter by anachronism. According to him, the action occurs at a time when the war in Flanders is raging and wine is being produced in Burgundy and Orléans.

The comparison between the age of fable and contemporary customs works in both directions, since not only is a literary convention ridiculed, but also modern customs are satirized as seen through these fictional characters: witness the meeting of the council of the gods which may be applied to such sessions in France of the seventeenth century, or even to many such sessions today. Although the gods finally defeat the barbarian giants, the question is raised by this poem of the decadence of luxury and the energy of primitivism. Could Scarron have been referring in the poem to the French court? It is a possibility. The poem is dedicated to Mazarin, and refers also to the king:

> *Que de très-adorable corps*
> *De nostre Royne, que tant j'aime,*
> *Sortit Louis quatorzième,*
> *Louys surnommé Dieu-donné,*
> *Pour le bien de la France né,*
> *Qui secondé de ta prudence*
> *Nous mettra dans l'abondance,*
> *En dépit ces maudits Géants.*

(From the very worthy body/of our queen whom I love so dearly,/came forth Louis the fourteenth,/Louis also named God-given,/born for the good of France,/He who seconds your prudence/will lead us to abundance/despite the cursed giants.) (Bk. I, p.4)

The dedication to the poem then actually compares the king and his court to the Olympian gods, threatened by the evil giants. Mazarin will help the king dispose of the threat and lead France to abundance. This comparison per se is very flattering; but if taken in the context of the poem, can in turn create a ridiculous court. The manners and customs described in the poem are certainly not those of gods (notice that Louis XIV is referred to as *Dieudonné*) or what a description of the court should be.

It is known that Mazarin did not reply to Scarron's plea for assistance. He may have been aware of the burlesque implications of the poem. If this is true, and Scarron had these intentions in mind, it would then not be very difficult to explain the *Mazarinade* published a few years later; after all, the battle which this poem predicts would then have come to pass through the Fronde. In fact, the analogy of a person in power as Jupiter is preserved at a certain point in the *Mazarinade,* as Gautier points out. After an adventure with a fruit vendor, "Mazarin flees by foot and with little flourish to Barcelona from whence he returns to his country as he is able, there to begin again his life by holding the place of Ganimides in the service of a scarlet Jupiter [Richelieu]."[3] The political implications then, of *Typhon,* may be of interest in the study of the writings of Paul Scarron.

III *Virgil Travestied*

Although many of Scarron's contemporaries regarded his *Virgile travesti* as the poet's major contribution, it is hardly read today. If the modern reader is interested in an example of the burlesque in Scarron he will turn to the *Typhon,* which is much shorter and much more readable and where social satire is clearly evident. It would be very easy to tire of the extremely long and careful travesty of the *Aeneid* of Virgil. Indeed, Scarron did just that: he never finished the work, for he tired of it. He also had doubts about the genre he had popularized: Book V attests to both of these reasons for not completing his work. It should also be remembered that Scarron did not object to Père Vavasseur's invective against the burlesque, but actually agreed with his *De ludicra dictione.*

In the *Virgile travesti* we see an author who is using the tastes of the time to improve his position. He does not enjoy the creation of a burlesque poem; yet his facility for the burlesque and the demands of the public encourage him to continue the work which he would never attempt to finish. This is very different from the *Roman comique* of which he was so proud and on which he continued work until his death.

For the sources of Scarron's inspiration, it is possible to look to Italy: it has already been pointed out that as a general rule Scarron derives his burlesque inspiration from that country while his romanesque derives from beyond the Pyrenees. When Scarron went to Italy, it is possible that he met Giovanni Battista Lalli, who was living in Rome and had composed in 1633 a *Virgil Travestied.* He may have also heard of other precursors of the burlesque such as Pulci, with his *Morgante maggiore,* or of Berni de Lamporecchio, who composed a parody of Boiardo's *Orlando inamorato.*

Why did Scarron choose the *Aeneid* as the subject of his travesty? Simply because it was the most sublime of all works to his contemporaries. It should be recalled that this was a Classical age, and

imitation of the ancients was regarded as proper procedure in
the creation of a work of art. The epic was one of the recognized
forms as stated by Aristotle and restated by all Neoclassical theorists,
and it was the *Aeneid* in this period that stood as the example of
the Classical epic: in the short period from 1603 to 1639 the *Aeneid*
was translated into French at least twelve times. Thus, Virgil's work
stood as the sublime model and invited travesty. Already Sorel in
his *Francion* had noticed the extremes to which people went in
the praise and imitation of this poem, and had Hortensius, the
evil schoolmaster, state that Virgil holds the knowledge of all
ages—did he not lead Dante in the *Divine Comedy?*

If Scarron wanted to be master of the burlesque, he then had to
use Virgil as a model and change into comical what was regarded
as sublime. Although Boileau did not approve of the burlesque
and banished *Typhon* (he did not mention the *Virgile travesti*)
to the countryside, where people like the *précieuses ridicules* could
read it, the work seems to have pleased many defenders of Classicism. Georges de Scudéry, for example, states: "Virgil himself
would laugh/to see himself so well masked."[4]

Other authors like Boisrobert, Segrais, and even Racine enjoyed
reading the travesty. Indeed, in spite of Boileau's condemnation,
the theoretician of Classicism seems to have used similar techniques
in his mock-heroic poem *Le Lutrin* to those used by Scarron.[5]

The techniques used by Scarron in the creation of this burlesque
poem are very similar to those he had already employed in *Le
Typhon*. For example, the French poet uses trivial details to debase
the high tone of the epic. These details usually link the heroes
of antiquity to the bourgeoisie of seventeenth-century Paris. Thus,
anachronism is brought in also. It should be recalled that in *Typhon*
Scarron had treated the gods as *bourgeois*. Here is an example of
this double technique as quoted by Gaston Hall:

> *Je chante cet homme pieux*
> *Qui vint chargé de tous ses Dieux*
> *Et de Monsieur son père Anchise,*
> *Beau vieillard à la barbe grise,*
> *Depuis la ville où les Grégois*
> *Occirent tant de bons bourgeois . . .*

(I sing of this pious man/who came loaded down with all his gods/and
with Mister Anchise his father/a lovely old man with a white beard,/from
the town where the Greeks/killed so many fine bourgeois.)[6]

Another example of comical anachronism mentioned by Hall occurs in the description of a nymph:

> *Elle entend, et parle fort bien*
> *L'espagnol et l'italien,*
> *Le Cid du poète Corneille*
> *Elle le récite à merveille,*
> *Coude en linge en perfection,*
> *Et sonne cu psaltérion.*

(She controls as well as one could wish/Italian and Spanish,/she recites to our marvel/the *Cid* of the poet Corneille,/sews her linen ever so perfectly/and plays the dulcimer correctly.)[7]

In addition to these two techniques already found in *Typhon,* the French poet, according to Morillot, has a particular vision of life in the burlesque: "Like La Rochefoucauld, he only saw egotism and self-love around him."[8]

Thus, as in *Typhon,* the base motives for high actions are discussed. In the previous poem, the war had started with a game of ninepins and the destruction of Jupiter's glasses. Here, the wrath of Juno is exposed in its pettiness, and the love of Dido for Aeneas is also ridiculed in Book IV. Charles Cotton, who translated this poem into English calling it *Scarronides or Virgil Travestie,* a mock-poem, begins Book IV as follows:

> *In this Fourth book we find it written,*
> *That Dido Queen was deeply smitten;*
> *Much taken with the Trojan's person,*
> *Than which a proper was scarce one:*
> *Much of his Breeding did she reckon;*
> *A Braver Man ne'er handled Weapon;*
> *This caused her tender Heart to flame,*
> *She vow'd she'd have him, though to her shame.*[9]

We can almost imagine the students in *Francion* reading with great pleasure these lines after having had instruction from the pedantic Hortensius. This type of reaction may account for the great popularity that the poem enjoyed in the seventeenth century.

IV Léandre et Héro

Returning to satire of sublime models, Scarron published in 1656 his *Léandre et Héro*. The techniques found in this poem are very similar to those found in *Typhon* and in *Virgile travesti*. However, Robert Berens finds that there has been an evolution: "The later work is more artistically done and more eloquently expressed. The frequent lyrical moments, the touches of true sensitivity and the statements by Scarron on what a poem should and should not be give it a place of great importance in our study of Scarron as a literary satirist."[10] The careful consideration given by Berens to the poem renders a detailed analysis of this work unnecessary. It is regretful, however, that the author did not consider the sources of the poem in his discussion of it. Although it has been stated that Scarron derived his poem from one by Clément Marot, Gustave Lanson has shown that the model for this poem came from Spain. Scarron used Luis de Góngora's *Romance* of Hero and Leander. Indeed some of the examples quoted by Berens to show Scarron's burlesque techniques are derived from the Spanish. For example, while at a temple during a sacrificial service, Hero's father falls asleep and snores loudly. This comic incident is found in both versions.[11]

Yet, the comical incidents, some taken from the Spanish and others created by the burlesque genius of Scarron, seem to disappear as the story progresses. At some points, as stated by Berens, Scarron becomes sincerely tender. As the lovers part, and the reader knows it is for the last time, the burlesque poet states:

> *Je laisse à juger aux lecteurs*
> *Quand ces amants se séparèrent*
> *Si leurs coeurs tendres soupirèrent*
> *Si leurs yeux versèrent des pleurs.*

(I leave it up to the readers to decide/when these lovers parted/whether or not their tender hearts heaved sighs/whether or not tears streamed from their eyes.)[12]

At first glance, this appears to be the same technique as employed for example in the *Roman comique* for comical effect. There the author, when attempting to ridicule the language of lovers, leaves the reader to *imagine* all the beautiful phrases. Here, what we imagine is not the long speeches that Scarron satirized in other works.

In fact, he had just stated that they must part *sans cérémonie*.[13] Thus, the simplicity of their departure matched by the simple and concise statements of the poet brings out the utter powerlessness of the lovers when confronted by their destiny. There is nothing they can say in the immensity of their love and their fate. The Léandre that had previously fallen from his mare into the mud now becomes a truly romanesque figure. Yet, this image is not maintained to the end, where Scarron ridicules the sadness of Hero, and thus relieves the tension created by tragedy.

Berens notes that after the publication of *Léandre et Héro* the poetry of Scarron developed more and more away from the burlesque. He notes that in 1658–59 he wrote six *épitres chagrines* in which no trace of burlesque remains. Thus, it is possible to see in the poetry also a kind of evolution away from the burlesque and toward the romanesque. Yet, this evolution came in the poetry later than in other forms. Thus, the evidence for it is scant and can be found only in the last four years of the poet's life. As stated before, the reason for this is possibly that Scarron's poetry was mainly intended to bring him remuneration. It is incidental by nature and thus relies more heavily on wit than on romanesque qualities.

In conclusion, then, there can be gleaned in his poetry the kind of evolution found in the other forms. This evolution should caution the reader and the critic in referring to Scarron only as a representative of the burlesque in reaction to the *préciosité* of his times.

Conclusion

Paul Scarron, the poet of the burlesque, is indeed a man who, persecuted by fortune, lashed out against it with satire and invective. Yet this alone does not do justice to the man or to his works. In addition to laughter and criticism, we have found in the writings of the Queen's Invalid a persistent interest in the romanesque. His masterpiece, the *Roman comique,* written at a mature age, contains a pleasing balance between the comical and the ideal.

The French poet derived his formula from Spain. *Don Quijote* served as a model for the *Roman comique,* while the Spanish *comedia* had great influence on his theater: the blending of the serious, the ideal, with the laughter of the *gracioso* reminded Scarron of Cervantes' ambivalent attitude toward the Knight of La Mancha.

This formula, although always present, evolved slowly. It can be stated that Scarron's early works rely mainly on the comical, while, as time went on, his writings became more and more romanesque. In his voyage toward this ideal realm, Scarron was guided not only by Spanish literary works but also by two people who exerted great influence on his life: Cabart de Villermont and his wife Françoise d'Aubigné.

It has been our purpose to show the importance of this progression in the life and works of a man, synonymous with the burlesque.

Notes and References

(All translations are the author's
unless otherwise indicated)

Chapter One

1. Pierre Gaxotte, *Histoire des Français* (Paris: Flammarion, 1951).

2. An interesting description of Henry IV's funeral and its relation to Scarron can be found in Naomi F. Phelps's *The Queen's Invalid* (Baltimore: The Johns Hopkins Press, 1951), pp. 1–3.

3. Phelps, *Queen's Invalid,* p. 11.

4. Some of these biographers are: Henri Chardon, J.J. Jusserand, Raymond R. MacCurdy, and Emile Magne.

5. Emile Magne in *Scarron et son milieu* (Paris: Emile-Paul, 1924), p. 7, calls these years "son apprentissage de burlesque" and blames the counselor as much as the stepmother.

6. A vivid description of the schools of the time is given by Charles Sorel in *Le Francion.*

7. This statement by Cosnac is quoted by Henri Chardon in *Scarron inconnu* (Paris: Champion, 1904), p. 11.

8. Magne, *Scarron,* p. 9. However, the poems dedicated to these ladies are dated by Maurice Cauchie in the 1640's. This would place these attachments on his return to Paris from Le Mans.

9. Théophile Gautier, *Les Grotesques* (Paris: Michel Lévy Freres, 1859), p. 342.

10. Later, in 1651, Scarron dedicated the first part of the *Roman comique* to him in the hope of receiving a *bénéfice.*

11. Maynard was a disciple of Malherbe, Scarron's favorite poet, and he also enjoyed the good life. Such common bonds resulted in a friendship that lasted throughout their lives.

12. Chardon, *Scarron,* p. 24. Magne, *Scarron,* pp. 43–44. Paul Morillot, *Scarron et le genre burlesque* (Paris: Lecène et Oudin, 1888), p. 15. Phelps, *Queen's Invalid,* p. 41.

13. G. Margouliès, "Scarron et Lope de Vega" *Revue de littérature comparée,* VIII (1928), pp. 512–13.

14. Magne, *Scarron,* pp. 43–44.

15. Phelps, *Queen's Invalid,* p. 41.

16. Margouliès, "Scarron et Lope de Vega," pp. 512–13.

17. Discussing this sonnet, María Rosa Lida de Malkiel states in "Para las fuentes españolas de algunos sonetos burlescos de Scarron," *Revue de littérature comparée*, XXVII (1953), p. 186: "Sin duda P. Morillot se equivocaba de hecho cuando, olvidado de la identificación de Ménage, creía que el *Sonnet du coude* emanaba de la experiencia personal de Scarron —de su viaje a Roma en 1635—."

18. According to Magne's biography of Scarron (p. 42), Fréart would later become one of the most dogmatic of the theoreticians that favored Classical art.

19. J.J. Jusserand, Introduction to *The Comical Romance and Other Tales* (London: Lawrence and Bullen, 1892), p. vii.

20. Jusserand, *Comical Romance*, p. vii.

21. Jusserand, *Comical Romance*, p. vii.

22. H. d'Alméras, *Le Roman comique de Scarron* (Paris: Societé Française d'éditions littéraires et techniques, 1931), pp. 22–23.

23. Magne in his biography of Scarron discusses at length Scarron's possible adventures and names Mlle Coquille as one of the poet's mistresses.

24. Magne, *Scarron*, pp. 53–54.

25. Phelps, *Queen's Invalid*, p. 50.

26. Phelps, *Queen's Invalid*, p. 51.

27. Tallemant des Réaux, *Historiettes* (Paris: Librairie Gallimard, 1960), p. 680.

28. Magne, *Scarron*, p. 78.

29. Chardon, *Scarron*, p. 70.

30. Victor Fournel, *La littérature indépendante et les écrivains oubliés* (Paris: Didier, 1862).

31. Morillot, *Scarron*, p. 138.

32. Robert Berens, *Aspects of Literary Satire in Sorel, Scarron and Furetière*, Diss. (Colorado, 1966), p. 19.

33. Phelps, *Queen's Invalid*, p. 79.

34. Phelps, *Queen's Invalid*, p. 79.

35. Charles Girauld, ed., *Oeuvres mêlées de Saint-Evremond* (Paris: J. Leon Techener, 1865), Vol. 2, p. 539.

36. Phelps states that the play was presented in 1643, but Magne gives the date of presentation as 1645.

37. On the subject of the *Mazarinade* see Phelps, *Queen's Invalid*, pp. 116–47; and Morillot, *Scarron*, pp. 220–37.

38. For a definition of the term "romanesque" see Berens, *Satire*, p. 178; and Antoine Adam, *Histoire de la littérature française au XVII siècle* (Paris: Editions Mondiales, 1962), Vol. 2, p. 331. In Scarron, the romanesque is a blend of the qualities found in the Spanish *comedia de capa y espada*, and the qualities found in the Greek romances. He, however,

dislikes some of the characteristics of the heroic romances in France, particularly their lack of verisimilitude, and relationship to the *précieux*.

39. According to Morillot, the *Relation véritable* was meant as a burlesque on Sarrasin's *Pompe funèbre* also written in memory of Voiture. However, according to Maurice Cauchie, Sarrasin's poem was not published until 1649.

40. Maurice Cauchie, ed., *Poésies diverses de Paul Scarron* (Paris: Société des textes français modernes, 1947), pp. 364–65.

41. Charles Augustin Sainte-Beuve, *Causeries du Lundi* (Paris: Garnier Frères, 1862), Vol. 4, p. 371.

42. Magne, *Scarron,* p. 172.

43. Magne, *Scarron,* p. 173.

44. Tallemant, *Historiettes,* Vol. 2, p. 1445.

45. Raymond R. MacCurdy, "The Theater of Paul Scarron and the Spanish Comedia," thesis, (Louisiana State University, 1941), p. 15.

46. MacCurdy, *Scarron,* p. 17.

47. The second part of the *Roman comique* was apparently finished in 1654 since at this time it was sold to Guillaume de Luyne. However, it was not actually published until 1657.

48. Guillaume de Luyne was Scarron's new publisher now that Toussant Quinet had died.

49. Phelps, *Queen's Invalid,* p. 223.

50. This play was produced at the end of 1654 but was not published until the following year. The production failed since Thomas Corneille had written an adaptation of the same play, which was a great success at that time.

51. Frédéric Lachèvre, *Scarron et sa gazette burlesque* (Paris: Giraud-Badin, 1929).

52. Lachèvre mentions *La Puttana errante* and *Creanza della donne* as possible sources.

53. Paul Scarron, *Oeuvres* (Paris: Jean François Bastien, 1786), Vol. 1, p. 141.

Chapter Two

1. An important study in this field is Maurice Magendie, *Le Roman français au XVII siècle* (Paris: Droz, 1932).

2. Antoine Adam, ed., *Romanciers du XVII siècle* (Paris: Gallimard, 1968), pp. 7–21.

3. An excellent study on this novelist is Frederick W. Vogler, *Vital d'Audiguier and the Early Seventeenth Century Novel* (Chapel Hill: University of North Carolina Press, 1964).

4. Consult Denis de Rougemont or C.S. Lewis on the subject.

5. Honoré d'Urfé, *L'Astrée* (Paris: Union Générale d'Editions, 1964), p. 119.

6. Antoine Adam lists another type which he considers as transitional between the sentimental and the heroic: the *roman d'aventures*. Here the hero is a purely imaginary creation and his adventures are fabulous as opposed to the historical setting of the heroic novels.

7. A short work to consult on the relationship of Petrarchism, Platonism, and chivalry is Leonard Forster, *The Icy Fire* (Cambridge: The University Press, 1969).

8. Allan H. Gilbert, ed., *Literary Criticism* (Detroit: Wayne State University Press, 1962), pp. 486–87.

9. There were, however, other changes made in *La Clélie* which can not be considered harmful. Antoine Adam points to Scudéry's modern conception of marriage and the role of women in the novel.

10. Dorothy Dallas, *Le Roman français de 1660 à 1680* (Paris: Gamber, 1932).

11. See Gustave Reynier, *Le Roman réaliste au XVII siècle* (Paris: Hachette, 1914).

12. George Saintsbury, *A History of the French Novel* (London: Macmillan, 1917), pp. 113–14.

13. Victor Fournel, ed., *Le Roman comique de Paul Scarron* (Paris: Bibl. Elzévirienne, 1857), p. vii.

14. Adam, *Romanciers*, p. 27.

15. Adam points to the recurring themes of generosity and liberty in Sorel's *Francion*.

16. Adam, *Histoire*, Vol. 2, p. 42.

17. Paul Scarron, *Comical Romance*, trans. by Tom Brown *et al.* (New York: Benjamin Blom, 1968), p. 3.

18. Scarron, *Comical Romance*, p. 30.

19. Adam, *Histoire*, Vol. 2, p. 145.

19. Adam, *Histoire*, Vol. 2, p. 145.

20. Paul Scarron, *Roman comique* in *Romanciers du XVII siècle*, Antoine Adam, ed. (Paris: Gallimard, 1968), p. 590.

21. Scarron, *Roman comique*, p. 604.

22. Scarron, *Roman comique*, p. 766.

23. Scarron, *Comical Romance*, p. 338.

24. Chardon, *Scarron*, Vol. 2, p. 272.

25. See Henri Chardon's *Scarron inconnu* and *La Troupe du "Roman comique" de Scarron dévoilée et les comédiens de campagne au XVII siècle* (Le Mans: Typographie Edmond Monnoyer, 1876).

26. Adam, *Histoire*, Vol. 2, p. 145.

27. Chardon, *Scarron*, Vol. 2, pp. 190–209.

28. Reynier, *Roman réaliste*, p. 277.

29. Paul Scarron, *Dernières oeuvres* (Paris: David père, Durand, Pissot, 1752), p. 47.

30. Reynier, *Roman réaliste*, p. 277.

31. Adolphe de Puibusque, *Histoire comparée des littératures espagnole et française* (Paris: Dentu, 1843), Vol. 2.

32. Reynier, *Roman réaliste,* p. 277.

33. Justo García Morales, ed., "Prólogo" to Agustín de Rojas, *El viaje entretenido* (Madrid: Aguilar, n.d.), p. 27.

34. For a careful examination of this question, see Ethel Vaughn, *"El viaje entretenido" by Agustín de Rojas: A Possible Source of "Le Roman comique,"* Diss. (Northwestern, 1929).

35. Maurice Bardon, *"Dom Quichotte" en France au XVII et au XVIII siècles* (Paris: Librairie Ancienne Honoré Champion, 1931), p. 96.

36. Bardon, *Dom Quichotte,* p. 99.

37. Myron L. Kocher, *A critical edition of "La Bibliothèque Françoise" of Charles Sorel,* Diss. (North Carolina, 1965), p. 341.

38. Nicolas Boileau, "Art poétique" in *Oeuvres de Boileau,* Jacques Bainville, ed. (Paris: Cité des livres, 1828), Vol. 1, p. 242.

39. Voltaire, *Siècle de Louis XIV* in *Oeuvres complètes* (Paris: Garnier, 1878), Vol. 14, p. 136.

40. Sainte-Beuve, *Lundis,* Vol. 12, p. 186.

41. Sainte-Beuve, *Lundis,* Vol. 12, p. 187.

42. Gautier, *Grotesques,* p. vi.

43. Gautier, *Grotesques,* pp. 336–37.

44. Gautier, *Grotesques,* p. 339.

45. Fournel, *Roman comique,* p. v.

46. Paul Bourget, "Préface" to Paul Scarron, *Roman comique* (Paris: Librairie des bibliophiles, 1880), pp. i–xxxii.

47. Relating Naturalism to the burlesque is essentially the same technique as that of Gautier who related the grotesque to the burlesque. These critics use new terms to describe what others have considered Scarron's main characteristic: his propensity for the burlesque.

48. André Le Breton, *Le Roman au XVII siecle* (Paris: Hachette, 1890), p. 98.

49. Ferdinand Brunetière, *Etudes critiques sur l'histoire de la littérature française* (Paris: Hachette, 1907), Vol. 4, pp. 57–94.

50. Reynier, *Roman réaliste,* p. 208.

51. Reynier, *Roman réaliste,* p. 208.

52. Magne, *Scarron,* p. 162.

53. R. Cadorel, *Scarron et la nouvelle espagnole dans le "Roman comique"* (Aix-en-Provence: La Pensée Universitaire, 1960), p. 6.

54. G. Hainsworth, *Les "Novelas exemplares" de Cervantes en France au XVII siècle* (Paris: Champion, 1933).

55. Roland Mortier, "La Fonction des nouvelles dans le *Roman comique,*" *Cahiers de l'association internationale des études françaises,* No. 18 (1966), p. 51.

56. Mortier, "Fonction des nouvelles," p. 50.

57. Ernest Simon, "The Function of the Spanish Stories in Scarron's *Roman comique," L'Esprit créateur,* III (1963), p. 133.

58. Simon, "Function of the Spanish stories," p. 134.

Chapter Three

1. Allan H. Gilbert, ed., *Literary Criticism: Plato to Dryden* (Detroit: Wayne State University Press, 1962), p. 575.

2. Gilbert, *Literary Criticism,* p. 575.

3. All text citations dealing with Georges de Scudéry's "Preface" to *Ibrahim* are from Gilbert, *Literary Criticism,* pp. 581–85.

4. The epic quality of the Greek romances and their relationship to the seventeenth century novel is perceptively discussed by Jean Boorsch in "About Some Greek Romances," *Yale French Studies,* XXXVII (1967), pp. 72–88.

5. All page references to Scarron's *Roman comique* and Offray's continuation will be from *The Comical Romance,* trans, Tom Brown *et al.* (New York: Benjamin Blom, 1968), unless otherwise stated.

6. Gilbert, *Literary Criticism,* p. 579.

7. Miguel de Cervantes, *Don Quijote de la Mancha,* Martin de Riquer, ed. (Barcelona: Editorial Juventud, 1967), Vol. 1, p. 31.

8. The goodness of fortune reveals a close relationship between the hero and a heavenly protector. Destin is always saved from anything which might destroy his idealism. In this, Scarron may have been following the example of the Greek romances; Boorsch in his revealing article states that such a distance existed in the works of fiction in antiquity: "to make the spectator feel that there is a net spread under the acrobatics of the protagonists, which will keep them from falling into bottomless depths of despair, into nauseous pits of abjection" (p. 83).

9. Frederick A. de Armas, *The Four Interpolated Stories in the "Roman comique"* (Chapel Hill: University of North Carolina Press, 1971).

10. This does not imply that Scarron objected to the idea of a salon or to conversation. It should be recalled that his *hôtel* could be considered a salon during the latter part of his life. Yet, the conversation there dealt with life and not with such remote topics as are discussed in the abbé Pure's *La Précieuse.*

11. Alonson de Castillo Solórzano, *Los alivios de Casandra* (Barcelona: Jayme Romeu, 1640), p. 63.

12. Castillo Solórzano, *Alivios,* p. 63.

13. Castillo Solórzano, *Alivios,* p. 43.

14. María de Zayas y Sotomayor, *Novelas ejemplares y amorosas* (Madrid: Aldus S.A. de Artes Gráficas, 1948), p. 162.

15. Castillo Solórzano, *Alivios,* p. 45.

16. Castillo Solórzano, *Alivios,* pp. 78–79.

17. Scarron, *Roman comique*, p. 555. The English translation differs from the French original. Davies translates the statement as "castles in the air" (p. 31), thus destroying the ironic reference.

18. Adam, *Histoire*, Vol. 2, pp. 147–48.

19. Some details which may have bearing on Scarron's political and religious attitudes can be found in the monumental work, *Ecrivains français en Hollande* by Gustave Cohen (Paris: Librairie Ancienne Edouard Champion, 1920).

20. Boorsch, "Greek Romances," p. 81.

21. Boorsch, "Greek Romances," pp. 72–88.

Chapter Four

1. S. E. Leavitt, *Scarron in England 1656–1800*. Diss. (Harvard, 1917).

2. Magne, *Scarron*, p. 185.

3. Emile Magne, *Bibliographie générale des oeuvres de Scarron* (Paris: Ancienne Librairie Leclerc L. Giraud-Badin, 1924), pp. 149–50. Previous to the publication of this bibliography, the *suite d'Offray* was thought to be of 1677.

4. Chardon, *Scarron*, pp. 268–366.

5. Adam, *Romanciers*, p. 41.

6. Adam, *Romanciers*, p. 800.

7. Adam, *Romanciers*, p. 41.

8. Fournel, *Roman comique*, p. lxxxiv.

9. Some information on this author is provided by Fernand Fleuret and Louis Perceau in their anthology, *Les Satires français au XVII siècle* (Paris: Garnier, 1923), Vol. 1, p. 184.

10. Some of the modern editions which include this continuation are those edited by Antoine Adam, Emile Magne, and Benjamin Boyce.

11. Scarron, *Roman comique*, p. 819.

12. Scarron, *Roman comique*, p. 880.

13. This is not always the case: Chapter IX is thoroughly amusing.

14. Adam, *Histoire*, Vol. 4, p. 164.

15. Fournel, *Roman comique*, p. lxxxiii.

16. This conclusion is summarized in the second volume of the *Bibliothèque universelle des romans*.

Chapter Five

1. Frédéric Deloffre, *La Nouvelle en France à l'age classique* (Paris: Didier, 1967), p. 11.

2. Jules Hasselmann, ed., *Les Conteurs français du XVI siècle* (Paris: Librairie Larousse, 1945), p. 6.

3. Deloffre, *Nouvelle,* p. 17.

4. Hainsworth, *Novelas exemplares,* p. 102.

5. Miguel de Cervantes, *Novelas ejemplares* (Buenos Aires: Editorial Sopena Argentina, 1962), p. 7.

6. See Caroline B. Bourland, *The Short Story in Spain in the Seventeenth Century* (Northampton: Smith College, 1927).

7. Kocher, *Bibliothèque françoise,* p. 324.

8. Dallas, *Roman français,* p. 152.

9. For further examples see Hainsworth, *Novelas exemplares,* p. 189.

10. Paul Scarron, *Nouvelles tragi-comiques* (Paris: Stock, 1948), p. 16.

11. Zayas, *Novelas,* p. 16. Scarron, *Nouvelles,* p. 12.

12. Scarron, *Nouvelles,* p. 60.

13. J. W. Coke in *Antoine Le Metel, Sieur d'Ouville: His Life and his Theater,* Diss. (Indiana, 1968), pp. 23–24, raises doubts about this statement. Although he accepts Tallemant des Réaux's information that d'Ouville spent seven years in Spain, he rejects Chardon's connection between d'Ouville and Dognon at this time, since he dates the trip around 1634 when Dognon was still a boy.

14. Chardon, *Scarron,* p. 325.

15. Hainsworth, *Novelas exemplares,* p. 194.

16. Chardon, *Scarron,* p. 326.

17. Lena E. V. Sylvania, *Doña Maria de Zayas y Sotomayor: A Contribution to the Study of Her Works* (New York: Columbia University Press, 1922), p. 22.

18. Chardon, *Scarron,* p. 332.

19. Chardon, *Scarron,* p. 337.

20. See Frank Sedwick, *A History of the Useless Precaution Plot in Spanish and French Literatures* (Chapel Hill: University of North Carolina Press, 1964).

21. Indeed, *La hija de Celestina* is included in a Spanish collection of picaresque novels edited by Angel Valbuena Prat. It is also discussed in Chandler's *Romances of Roguery.*

22. Adam, *Histoire,* Vol. 3, p. 298.

23. Adam, *Histoire,* Vol. 3, pp. 293–321.

24. John Davies of Kidwelly, trans., *Scarron's Novels* (London: Everingham, 1694), p. 125.

25. Zayas, *Novelas,* p. 293.

26. Davies, *Novels,* pp. 126–27.

27. Davies, *Novels,* p. 128.

28. Zayas, *Novelas,* p. 295.

29. See G. Hainsworth, "New Details on the *Nouvelles* of Scarron and Boisrobert," *Bulletin Hispanique,* XLIX (1947), pp. 145–69.

30. See J. H. Aronja, "The Case of Lope de Vega's *Amar, servir y esperar,*" *Romanic Review,* XLIV (1953), pp. 256–262.

31. Davies, *Novels,* p. 322.

32. Davies, *Novels,* p. 323.

33. Davies, *Novels,* p. 339. This translation is not very accurate. The French text states: "qui étoit depuis revenue à Naples pour des raisons que j'ignore et qui sont peu importantes au récit de cette histoire."

34. Davies, *Novels,* p. 291. The French version does not include the parentheses on vanity.

Chapter Six

1. On the theater see Ernest Martineche, *La comedia espagnole en France de Hardy à Racine* (Paris: Hachette, 1900); and Henry Carrington Lancaster, *A History of French Dramatic Literature in the Seventeenth Century* (Baltimore: Johns Hopkins, 1932).

2. Lancaster, *Dramatic Literature,* Pt. 3, Vol. 3, p. 430.

3. See J. W. Coke, *Antoine Le Metel, Sieur d'Ouville: His Life and His Theater,* Diss. (Indiana, 1968).

4. "Seroit-elle point soeur de nostre Esprit Folet?" Lancaster, *Dramatic Literature,* Pt. 3, Vol. 3, p. 431.

5. Scarron, *Roman comique,* p. 570.

6. Berens, *Literary Satire,* p. 186.

7. Berens, *Literary Satire,* p. 191.

8. Berens, *Literary Satire,* p. 192.

9. MacCurdy, *Scarron,* p. 100.

10. Lancaster, *Dramatic Literature,* Pt. 2, Vol. 2, p. 453.

11. Lancaster, *Dramatic Literature,* Pt. 2, Vol. 2, p. 466.

12. Dates in parentheses are dates of publication. This particular play was first presented in 1643.

13. Frederick W. Moore, *The Drama of Paul Scarron,* Diss. (Yale, 1956), p. 146.

14. Adam, *Histoire,* Vol. 3, p. 261.

15. Lancaster, *Dramatic Literature,* Pt. 2, Vol. 2, p. 465.

16. Berens, *Literary Satire,* p. 193.

17. Lancaster, *Dramatic Literature,* Pt. 2, Vol. 2, p. 466.

18. All textual citations of Scarron's plays in this chapter are from *Oeuvres de Scarron* (Paris: Chez Jean François Bastien, 1786), 7 Vols.

19. Alonso de Castillo Solórzano, *El Marqués de Cigarral* in *B. A. E.,* Vol. 45, p. 313.

20. Raymond MacCurdy, *Rojas Zorrila* (New York: Twayne, 1968), p. 67.

Chapter Seven

1. Scarron points to his source at the end of the poem when he states: "Et moy je mets fin à mon conte,/tiré du sieur Noelle Conte."

2. All text citations of the poem are from Paul Scarron, *Typhon* (Paris: Toussainct Quinet, 1644).

3. Gautier, *Grotesques*, p. 373.

4. Morillot, *Scarron*, p. 196.

5. This has been pointed out by H. Gaston Hall in his article "Scarron and the Travesty of Virgil," *Yale French Studies*, XXXVII (1967), pp. 115–27.

6. Hall, "Scarron," p. 119.

7. Hall, "Scarron," p. 121.

8. Morillot, *Scarron*, p. 196.

9. Charles Cotton, *Scarronides* (London: J. Galton, 1804), p. 54.

10. Berens, *Literary Satire*, pp. 169–70.

11. The following are examples of both the Spanish and French versions, taken from Gustave Lanson, "Littérature française et littérature espagnole au XVII siècle," *Revue d'Histoire littéraire de la France*, III (1896), pp. 326–31:

Cependent que dévotement
Sa mère prioit dans le temple,
Son père de mauvois example,
Sur un banc ronfloit rudement.

Señora madre, devota
se estuvo siempre rezando
y señor padre, poltrón,
se salió a dormir al claustro.

12. *Oeuvres de Scarron*, Vol. 7, p. 279.

13. *Oeuvres de Scarron*, Vol. 7, p. 279.

Selected Bibliography

This bibliography attempts to be as complete as possible on books, theses, and articles dealing *exclusively* with Paul Scarron. More general works are not included, but many are pointed out in the notes. Primary sources listed are only those utilized in this volume.

PRIMARY SOURCES

Oeuvres de Scarron. 7 Vols. Paris: Chez Jean François Bastien, 1786. All the main works of Scarron are included. The following is a list of the main entries in each volume. I: Portrait of Scarron, letters, and *Mazarinade.* II: *Roman comique.* III: Offray's and Préchac's continuations of the *Roman comique* and the *Nouvelles.* IV: *Virgile travesti.* V: Continuation of *Virgile travesti* and *Typhon.* VI: All the plays except for the fragments. VII: Short poems and fragments of comedies.

Roman comique in *Romanciers du XVII siècle,* edited by Antoine Adam. Paris: Gallimard, 1958.

Roman comique, edited by Henri Benac. Paris: Belles Lettres, 1951.

Roman comique, edited by Emile Magne. Paris: Garnier, 1955.

Typhon. Paris: Toussainct Quinet, 1644.

Translations into English:

Comical Romance, translated by Tom Brown *et al.* New York: Benjamin Blom, 1968.

Scarron's Novels, translated by John Davies of Kidwelly. London: Everingham, 1694. This work includes: "The Fruitless Precaution," "The Hypocrites," "The Innocent Adultery," "The Judge of Her Own Cause," "The Rival Brothers," "The Invisible Mistress," "The Chastisement of Avarice," and "The Unexpected Choice."

Scarronides. London: J. Galton, 1804. This is an adaptation of the *Virgile travesti* into English.

SECONDARY SOURCES

1. Books:

ALMÉRAS, H. D'. *Le "Roman comique" de Scarron.* Paris: Société française d'éditions littéraires et techniques, 1931. A short introduction to the genesis of the *Roman comique.*

158

BERENS, ROBERT. *Aspects of Literary Satire in Sorel, Scarron and Furetière.* Diss. Colorado, 1966. An essential work to consult in the study of Scarron's humor. His discussion of the poem *Léandre et Héro* is significant even though he does not take into account the sources of the poem. Like most critics, he does not pay much attention to the romanesque qualities in Scarron's works; yet, he is thorough in his analysis of humor.

CADOREL, R. *Scarron et la nouvelle espagnole dans le "Roman comique."* Aix-en-Provence: La Pensée Universitaire, 1960. The author states categorically that there are no relationships between the *nouvelles* and the rest of the novel. There are also inaccuracies in the discussion of sources. More than two thirds of the work is taken up with the French text of the stories and French translations of the Spanish tales.

CHARDON, HENRI. *La Troupe du "Roman comique" dévoilée et les comédiens de campagne au XVII siècle.* Le Mans: Typographie Edmond Monnoyer, 1876. The author proves that the troupe of Molière was not the one presented in Scarron's novel. Yet, his attempt to prove that it was the troupe of Filandre, according to Adam, has no more basis than the old legend.

————. *Scarron inconnu.* Paris: Champion, 1904. The author attempts to prove that Scarron had taken specific people of seventeenth-century Le Mans as characters in his novel. Although the work presents an interesting picture of that city during the time Scarron resided there, most of his correlations do not rest on solid ground.

DE ARMAS, FREDERICK A. *The Four Interpolated Stories in the "Roman comique": Their Sources and Unifying Function.* Chapel Hill: University of North Carolina Press, 1971. The sources of Scarron's *nouvelles* are pointed out, and the changes made by the French author are studied in relation to the whole novel.

JUSSERAND, J.J. *English Essays from a French Pen.* London: T.F. Unwin, 1895. This book contains an essay entitled "Paul Scarron" in which the author points to Scarron's admiration for Poussin.

LACHÈVRE, FRÉDÉRIC. *Scarron et sa gazette burlesque.* Paris: Giraud-Badin, 1929. This work adds some interesting details to the life of the burlesque poet.

LEAVITT, S.E. *Scarron in England 1656–1800.* Diss. Harvard, 1917. The French poet was much translated and imitated in England.

MacCURDY, RAYMOND R. "The Theater of Paul Scarron and the Spanish Comedia." Thesis, Louisiana State University, 1941. A detailed comparison.

MAGNE, EMILE. *Bibliographie générale des oeuvres de Scarron.* Paris: Ancienne Librairie Leclerc L. Giraud-Badin, 1924. The only bibliography of the works of Scarron. An essential book in the study of the French poet.

————. *Scarron et son milieu*. Paris: Emile-Paul, 1924. The most complete biography of Scarron.

MOORE, FREDERICK W. *The Drama of Paul Scarron*. Diss. Yale, 1956. The most up-to-date discussion of Scarron's theater.

MORILLOT, PAUL. *Scarron et le genre burlesque*. Paris: Lecène et Oudin, 1888. A detailed study of Scarron as head of the burlesque movement in France.

PHELPS, NAOMI F. *The Influence of Paul Scarron on Restoration Literature*. Diss. Yale, 1942.

————. *The Queen's Invalid*. The only biography of Scarron in English, and the only major work on the French poet in this language.

SECORD, ARTHUR W. *Robert Drury's Journal and Other Studies*. Urbana: University of Illinois Press, 1961. The work contains an essay, "Scarron's *Roman comique* and Its English Translators," which adds John Bulteel to the list of translators.

VAUGHN, ETHEL. *"El viaje entretenido" by Agustín de Rojas: A Possible Source of "Le Roman comique."* Diss. Northwestern, 1929. A detailed comparison.

2. Articles:

BOISLISLE, A. DE. "Paul Scarron et Françoise d'Aubigne," *Revue des questions historiques*, X (1893), pp. 86–144, and 389–443. Helpful in the understanding of their relationship.

HAINSWORTH, G. "New Details on the *Nouvelles* of Scarron and Boisrobert," *Bulletin hispanique*, XLIX (1947), pp. 145–69. Points to *Palabras y Plumas* as the possible source of "Plus d'effets que de paroles."

HALL, H. GASTON. "Scarron and the Travesty of Virgil," *Yale French Studies*, XXXVII (1967), pp. 115–27. A starting point in any discussion of humor in the poetry of Scarron.

LANSON, GUSTAVE. "Littérature française et littérature espagnole au XVII siècle," *Revue d'histoire littéraire de la France*, III (1896), pp. 326–31. Contains a comparison of Gongora's *Romance* and Scarron's *Léandre et Héro*. It calls for a re-examination of the term "burlesque."

LIDA DE MALKIEL, MARÍA ROSA. "Para las fuentes españolas de algunos sonetos burlescos de Scarron," *Revue de littérature comparée*, XXVII (1953), pp. 185–91. Points out that Scarron borrowed from Lope de Vega in the composition of several sonnets. It comments on Margouliès' article.

MARGOULIÈS, G. "Scarron et Lope de Vega," *Revue de littérature comparée*, VIII (1928), pp. 511–15. The author discovered that Scarron had imitated Lope de Vega in various sonnets.

MORTIER, ROLAND. "La Fonction des nouvelles dans le *Roman comique*." *Cahiers de l'association internationale des études françaises,* 8 (1966), pp. 41–51. One of the first discussions of the possible interaction between the novel and its interpolations.

SERRANO PONCELA, SEGUNDO. "Casamientos Engañosos," *Bulletin hispanique,* LXIV (1962), pp. 248–59. Compares "El castigo de la miseria" with "Le Châtiment de l'avarice."

SIMON, ERNEST. "The Function of the Spanish Stories in Scarron's *Roman comique,*" *Esprit createur,* III (1963), pp. 130–37. A perceptive discussion of the relationship of the "History of the Invisible Mistress" to the rest of the novel.

Index

163